D1478643

A King is Bound in the Tresses

Studies in Biblical Literature

Hemchand Gossai
General Editor

Vol. 6

PETER LANG
New York • Washington, D.C./Baltimore • Boston • Bern
Frankfurt am Main • Berlin • Brussels • Vienna • Canterbury

Ann Roberts Winsor

A King is Bound
in the Tresses

Allusions to the Song of Songs
in the Fourth Gospel

PETER LANG
New York • Washington, D.C./Baltimore • Boston • Bern
Frankfurt am Main • Berlin • Brussels • Vienna • Canterbury

Library of Congress Cataloging-in-Publication Data

Winsor, Ann Roberts.
A king is bound in the tresses: allusions to the
Song of songs in the Fourth Gospel / Ann Roberts Winsor.
  p. cm. — (Studies in biblical literature; v. 6)
Includes bibliographical references (p.   ).
1. Bible. N.T. John—Criticism, interpretation, etc. 2. Bible. O.T. Song
of Solomon—Criticism, interpretation, etc. I. Title. II. Series.
BS2615.2.W56   226.5'066—dc21   97-31543
ISBN 0-8204-3931-2
ISSN 1089-0645

Die Deutsche Bibliothek-CIP-Einheitsaufnahme

Winsor, Ann Roberts:
A king is bound in the tresses: allusions to the
song of songs in the fourth gospel / Ann Roberts Winsor.
–New York; Washington, D.C./Baltimore; Boston; Bern;
Frankfurt am Main; Berlin; Brussels; Vienna; Canterbury: Lang.
(Studies in biblical literature; Vol. 6)
ISBN 0-8204-3931-2

The paper in this book meets the guidelines for permanence and durability
of the Committee on Production Guidelines for Book Longevity
of the Council of Library Resources.

Printed in the United States of America

Contents

Editor's Preface

More than ever the horizons in biblical literature are being expanded beyond that which is immediately imagined; important new methodological, theological, and hermeneutical directions are being explored, often resulting in significant contributions to the world of biblical scholarship. It is an exciting time for the academy as engagement in biblical studies continues to be heightened.

This series seeks to make available to scholars and institutions, scholarship of a high order, and which will make a significant contribution to the ongoing biblical discourse. This series includes established and innovative directions, covering general and particular areas in biblical study. For every volume considered for this series, we explore the question as to whether the study will push the horizons of biblical scholarship. The answer must be yes for inclusion.

In this volume Ann Roberts Winsor has carefully and insightfully explored aspects of John 12 and 20 focusing on the literary allusion of the Song of Songs to several enigmatic and seemingly incomprehensible and misplaced words, phrases and actions. Appealing to the studies by literary theorists Ben-Porat and Riffaterre, the author engages in a thorough and persuasive argument for the role of the Song of Songs as an intertextual antecedent. This study will fill an important role and be undoubtedly be widely lauded.

The horizon has been expanded.

Hemchand Gossai
General Editor

Introduction

Despite centuries of scrutiny, portions of the Fourth Gospel accounts of Jesus' anointing at Bethany (Jn 12:1–8) and his resurrection appearance to Mary Magdalene (Jn 20:1,11–18) have resisted explanation and remained enigmatic. While the continuing challenge presented by these texts reflects the abiding genius of the stories themselves, it also results from rather pedestrian narrative difficulties. Historical-critical approaches to analysis of these stories have failed to elicit satisfactory explanations of such crucial details as Mary of Bethany's wiping the ointment on Jesus' feet with her hair (12:3) or Jesus' command to Mary Magdalene to stop touching him when the text does not describe any touching (20:17). Other curious Johannine features also give rise to elements of mystery in these considerably nuanced narratives.

This study resolves the mystery by demonstrating that the images, motifs, and vocabulary of the Song of Songs are the matrix for the Johannine anointing and resurrection appearance narratives. The Fourth Evangelist's allusions to the Song follow the intertextual practice characteristic of biblical narrative. The allusions "program" the texts in such a way that the anticipated reader inevitably connects them. Long before the Johannine narratives became the texts now familiar to us, the stories' audiences had heard them many times under diverse circumstances. Apparent gaps or redundancies in the overall accounts needed no explanation for early listeners, who may also have heard the stories in varying orders.[1] Moreover, those Johannine community members most directly responsible for the tradition behind the written narratives evidently based their oral version of the accounts on the Song.

Recent years have seen a decline in the virtually absolute reign of historical criticism in the study of biblical texts. While biblical exegetes must continue to take account of the indispensable historical-critical issues in the investigation of texts, there is increasing recognition that biblical texts are no more subject to exclusively "objective, scientific" investigation than are other works of literature or accounts of spiritual experience. Even the apparent resolution of pertinent exegetical issues may leave an investigator with a sense that there remains much about a biblical narrative that is unclear or puzzling. Ancient texts are subject to the additional frustration of physical damage, loss, or mistransmission of manuscripts, with the resulting persistent possibility that the text one is trying to decipher may not even be what the author composed. So the interpretive process may falter at the physical as well as at the intellectual level, and the would-be interpreter may be tempted to cite faulty redaction or textual corruption to explain a text whose meaning has eluded the standard critical strategies. Indeed, these very obstacles have been specified in regard to the Johannine texts considered here.

Frustration has influenced some of the changes in the approaches to biblical scholarship, but what was at first seen as a failure of scientific method has yielded increasingly to a perspective of opportunity. Recognizing the merits of alternative investigative tactics, scholars have begun to adopt innovative, multidimensional approaches to Scripture. New literary critical techniques have effectively transformed the study of poetry and fiction, often clarifying and deepening the texts' meaning. These techniques are increasingly being applied to biblical texts as well, often with remarkably felicitous results. In many cases the creative genius of the biblical writer has been acknowledged as more consequential than previously recognized. In some instances, as in this study, a literary critical approach reconciles problematic textual difficulties left unexplained by historical-critical techniques.

Dissatisfaction with the analyses offered by historical-critical approaches to these two Johannine narratives leads to consideration of alternative methods. In spite of the comprehensive application of standard critical techniques to study of the Johannine accounts of Jesus' anointing and his resurrection appearance to Mary Magdalene, several points in those narratives appear inconsistent or even absurd at the logical level. At the intuitive level, however, they generate an intrinsic sense of communication. Both narratives exhibit an internal consistency, which the uncritical—or better, pre-critical—reader senses instinctively, but which is apparently not attainable through the usual historical-critical methods. The task is to learn what the stories mean on their own terms—retaining the enigmatic portions and articulating the reader's intuitive perception that these texts are meaningful as they stand.

The effectiveness of literary approaches to recalcitrant biblical texts suggests these techniques for Jn 12:1–8 and 20:11–18. The narrative qualities of these Johannine stories, as well as their immediate verbal and thematic connections with the Song of Songs, reinforce the appropriateness of a literary analysis. The intertextual strategies that characterize biblical narrative suggest the use of a critical method that encourages recognition of literary design. There are a number of well-conceived and provocative literary critical approaches now used in the service of interpretation of both secular and biblical texts.[2] I have chosen to use the critical work of modern literary theorists Michael Riffaterre and Ziva Ben-Porat because their studies focus specifically on evidence that allusion and intertextuality are integral components of the imaginative process. These two critics offer accounts of the process by which authors effect intertextual connections, as well as the goals of such links. The techniques they describe are largely applicable to narrative biblical texts, and modified versions of their work are effective tools for study of Jn 12 and 20.

The enigmas of Jn 12:1–8 and 20:11–18 that have not been resolved by the use of historical-critical methods invite a new approach to these texts, which includes relevant elements of the theories of Riffaterre and Ben-Porat. A detailed description of the narrative problems found in Jn 12:1–8 and close study of the text show how an understanding of the process of literary allusion virtually requires the reader to make the textual connections programmed into the narrative. The Johannine anointing account alludes specifically to the Song of Songs and, according to the workings of the poetics of allusion, the Evangelist continually guides the reader to make the connection with the Song. A similar process in regard to the story recounted in Jn 20:11–18 demonstrates that enigmas in the resurrection appearance story also point to allusions to the Song. Investigation of the Song as evoked text verifies that it is the referent to which the Evangelist alludes. Finally, the allusions to the Song are shown to be in keeping with the values and social context of the Johannine community.

The investigation's conclusions suggest areas of further study about the source of the stories and the constituency responsible for their telling. Inevitably, a reader who becomes aware of the allusions to the Song in the two Johannine narratives will also be drawn to consider the links between these Johannine stories, as well as their connection with the account of the raising of Lazarus. That story's early, proleptic reference to Mary of Bethany as Jesus' anointer makes clear that the accounts are to be seen together.

Allusion is a dynamic technique that gains impetus through each newly revealed implication, bringing new connections into its frame of reference and suggesting new textual relationships. Like the spiral that is never exhausted, the allusive process circles through portions of the old knowledge on its way farther up. It continues to invite expanding reflection on the issues generated by relational implications, suggesting insights into deeper intertextual layers and hints about the community sources of the narratives.

Notes

1   According to Margaret Davies, "Once we recognize that the Fourth Gospel *retells* a story already familiar to readers, we are no longer puzzled by the many gaps" (*Rhetoric and Reference in the Fourth Gospel* [Sheffield: JSOT Press, 1992]: 30). Davies includes the Evangelist's "premature" reference to Mary of Bethany as Jesus' anointer (Jn 11:2) before the anointing is described (Jn 12:3) among the clues to the audience's familiarity with the narrative.

2   For a summary of prominent recent theories, see the narrative-critical study of I. R. Kitzberger, "Mary of Bethany and Mary of Magdala—Two Female Characters in the Johannine Passion Narrative," (*New Testament Studies* 41 [1995]: 564–586). Kitzberger focuses on the literary *characterization* of these two women in the Fourth Gospel.

Chapter 1

Literary Allusion and Biblical Intertextuality

Mary of Bethany anointed Jesus' feet with ointment and *wiped his feet with her hair* (Jn 12:3); Mary Magdalene—after she *turned* (Jn 20:14) and *turned* (20:16)—was told by Jesus, "*do not hold me*" (20:17). Something seems awry. In the first instance, the action described is simply perplexing. In the second, the double turning confuses the reader about the precise nature of Mary's posture, and the "do not hold me" command is a non sequitur. How does one explain these bewildering elements of otherwise plausible narratives? In the study of biblical literature, it is always possible to conjecture that the text itself is corrupt or inaccurately edited. And indeed, theories of faulty redaction or possible textual *lacunae* have dominated scholarly assessment of these troublesome verses.[1] There is, however, another approach that takes seriously the literary integrity of the texts and assumes that the author deliberately created them as they are. The Johannine writer, as skilled as any modern author, may intend to lead the reader towards a camouflaged textual layer, or to appeal to an otherwise inaccessible imaginative realm. Approaches based on literary theory, especially those theories associated with Riffaterre and Ben-Porat, widen the exploratory scope for these verses as well as for the other parts of the Johannine anointing and resurrection appearance narratives. They also clarify aspects of these texts that older historical-critical techniques have failed to explain.

In the introductory chapter, I stated that the Johannine anointing at Bethany and resurrection appearance accounts are intertextually related to the Song of Songs. By allusive reference to the Song matrix, the Fourth Evangelist demonstrates awareness of composing within a tradition, maintaining the perception of the constant *presence* of the past.[2] Although the writer was not consciously composing "scripture," the Gospel's presentation of the life of Jesus as the continuation of God's saving presence in history connects the Johannine narrative to the biblical intertextual tradition and demonstrates the Evangelist's participation in the Jewish scriptural tradition. Because the focus here is on a *literary* matrix, the "biblical" nature of the New Testament is irrelevant.[3]

In the stories studied here, Jesus is presented as a compassionate and surprising human being whose behavior frequently perplexes. The characters with whom Jesus interacts also behave enigmatically and their behavior as well as his has confounded centuries of readers. The puzzling portions of the Jn 12:1-8 and 20:1,11-18 narratives are recognizable as examples of semiotic theorist Michael Riffaterre's "semantic indirection," which "threatens the literary representation of reality" by displacing, distorting, or creating meaning.[4] Riffaterre's insights clarify the method of the Fourth Evangelist by illuminating the textual creation process: the writer intends to guide the reader in a particular direction. Riffaterre emphasizes that it is the most precise descriptions whose departure from normal structures "make the shift toward symbolism more conspicuous."[5] An "ungrammaticality" refers to a textual enigma, the phenomenon that causes reader input as well as reader confusion. Although an ungrammaticality is literally an instance of deviant grammar, Riffaterre's use of the term covers any textual circumstance in which there is a "glitch," a situation where the reader feels that he or she has missed something, that the details are contradictory, that the text does not make sense. The ungrammaticalities occur because of a contradiction in terms, that is, a description generated by an expression that should exclude it.[6] The author's description may simply be inconsistent with verisimilitude or with what the reader might reasonably expect from the context. In order to be affected by the deviance from the norm, the reader must have already accepted the author's presentation of reality. The ungrammaticalities are stumbling blocks whose meaning becomes clear only at a deeper level of reading; although they seem to obscure, they are the key to understanding.[7] A textual ungrammaticality signifies that somewhere else, in another system, there is a grammaticality. The poetic sign is "textually ungrammatical, intertextually grammatical."[8]

Adapting this theory to the study of biblical narratives means that the discovery of an incomprehensible portion of text indicates that in another place—in a referent text—the apparent nonsense becomes logical. There are ungrammaticalities in the Johannine verses described above, in Mary of Bethany's wiping the ointment on Jesus' feet with her hair (Jn 12:3), and in Mary Magdalene's "turning" and then "turning" again as she converses with Jesus (Jn 20:14 and 16), as well as in Jesus' command that she not touch him when there is no indication that she has done so (20:17). The unusual use of hair, the repeated turning, and the ostensibly unmotivated command are signs that are notable because of their semantic indirection. The textual description is unrealistic at the first (*heuristic*) level of reading. In order to detect inconsistencies, the reader must be attentive to biblical writing practice and recognize that a supposed ungrammaticality in Scripture may simply reflect the literary style of the period. But one must also hesitate before discounting a textual "glitch" that in a modern work would signal a difficulty. The alert reader becomes aware that an unusual text is not a mistake, but a reference to another text, requiring one to seek a new relational paradigm.

While Riffaterre's goal in discerning semantic indirection is to discover the "semiotic" layer, the symbolic level of the poem, my investigation moves in another direction. Discovery of an ungrammaticality may signal the presence of a literary allusion in which the "symbol" will be another text. The second interpretive step then requires the reader to determine the referent text, recognizable because of its verbal or thematic similarities to the incomprehensible text, but not self-evident. Ziva Ben-Porat's theory of literary allusion describes the nature of the referent text and how to discern its identity. Ben-Porat's studies of the poetics of allusion emphasize the codifiable aspects of the technique and stress the author's intentionality. Literary allusions, she says, are not just hints or indirect references, but deliberate attempts to draw one text into relationship with another. Citing the vast number of allusions and the scarcity of explicit theories about allusion, Ben-Porat undertakes a discussion of that phenomenon as a literary device, asserting that

> the literary allusion is a device for the simultaneous activation of two texts. The activation is achieved through the manipulation of a special signal: a sign (simple or complex) in a given text characterized by an additional larger 'referent.' This referent is always an independent text. The simultaneous activation of the two texts thus connected results in the formation of intertextual patterns whose nature cannot be predetermined.[9]

Ben-Porat differentiates between intertextuality as a concept covering all relations between a given text and other texts, preceding or contemporaneous, and rhetorical intertextuality, whose function is to lead one to perceive the relation between particular texts.[10] Ben-Porat acknowledges that all concepts of allusion are based on a notion of indirect reference in one text to another, and that a rhetorical strategy in the author's design is characteristic of allusion as a technique. Indeed, Johannine references to the Song of Songs further distinct theological and social aims, as well as expressing the community's affection for the Song.

The device that provokes the allusion is the "marker," whose function is similar to Riffaterre's ungrammaticality: it is that word or phrase that indicates to the reader that another text is referred to. Ben-Porat says that as a built-in directional signal,

> the marker is always identifiable as an element or pattern belonging to another independent text. . . . In terms of the end product, the formation of intertextual patterns, the marker—regardless of the form it takes—is used for the activation of independent elements from the evoked text.[11]

The evoked text is not referred to directly. Even though the markers may be highly transparent, the evoked elements in the referent text require identification and, especially, activation before their full effect is felt. Recognition of the marker and identification of the evoked text begin the working out of the allusion's purpose and the reader's goal. The allusion's full contribution becomes apparent only as its ramifications are clarified in the formation of intertextual patterns. Simply identifying the marker and the text to which it refers does not address the substantive point of the author's use of allusion as a literary device. The reader cannot merely exchange the now discerned referents one for the other, but instead starts the complex process of actualizing the literary allusion, which, according to Ben-Porat, starts with the recognition of the marker and ends with intertextual patterning.[12]

Once a marker is noticed and the text it evokes is identified, the principal work of the allusion begins. Sometimes simply identifying the marked text suffices to complete the allusion. Occasionally the initial stages of recognition and identification of the marker and its object may be sufficiently perplexing to constitute a serious interpretive step, as in the case with the texts studied here. However, discernment of the Johannine allusions to the Song requires more than locating corresponding vocabulary. The markers must also concur thematically within the Song of Songs, and the allusions' plausibility must be substantiated within the social context of the Fourth Gospel community. With the exception of "search for the beloved" theme in Jn 20, Johannine allusions to the Song have been overlooked or disregarded in the past, so their presence is not apparent to post-Johannine readers.

When the reader recognizes the marker and then the marked or evoked text, the allusion process moves to the third stage. Recognition of the textual relationship invites an initial interpretation in which an intertextual pattern begins to be revealed. The reader modifies the "local interpretation" of the alluding word or phrase so that the marker (Riffaterre's ungrammaticality) is now understood differently within the text. It is no longer simply puzzling or interesting, but begins to be understood as the bearer of an alluding message. Recognizing this difference, the interpreter begins to note a nuanced change in perception because the context is now different. While a general allusion could be complete once the evoked text is identified, the literary allusion moves the reader deeper, stirring up a reaction to both the marker and the marked texts, as well as to both their contexts. The goal of a literary allusion takes shape as all the elements of both the alluding and evoked texts begin to interact with each other. The initial intertextual pattern generates new patterns so that increasing relationship develops among all portions of the alluding and evoked texts, no longer just those directly involved with the marker word. In this way, a metonymic textual affinity is implied, that is, an affinity between the *entire* alluding and evoked texts generated by the original allusion but surpassing it. Ben-Porat suggests that the interpretation of an evoked text that is historically hundreds of years earlier than the alluding text may be modified by its interaction with the later text. At this last stage of the allusive relationship, there need no longer be any continuum with the initial intertextual pattern.

The *literary* allusion, as Ben-Porat stresses, uses the elements of an independent text to "enrich and amplify the text in which it is manipulated. Its actualization is a process of approaching the maximal potential fullness of a text."[13] It is not only unrelated texts that are linked by allusion, for literary allusion may intensify the connection between texts that already share a relationship. Ben-Porat explains that the only common element in initially unrelated texts is the marker that generates analogies between reconstructed patterns. In contrast, initially related texts share many major components that act as markers. When texts already share a relationship, the markers result from the link between them rather than cause the link. The Fourth Gospel and the Song of Songs are initially *related* texts since they share world components and have in common major elements in their "fictional" worlds which act as markers. The alluding text (Jn) is a continuation of the referent text (SS). Even so, their lack of a definitively established connection makes it necessary to treat them like unrelated texts whose components would not be shared without the allusions.

One further item needs to be addressed, the emphasis on the para-doxically *restrictive* function of intertextuality. Riffaterre emphasizes that once the association signaled by the ungrammaticality is made, once the text under investigation is connected with its evoked text, the reader is no longer free to interpret the text however he or she wishes. The author intentionally moves the reader toward perception of an evoked text by means of allusive clues. Riffaterre asserts that the work's embeddedness in another text creates a "new hierarchy" which becomes difficult to ignore. "The reader's freedom of interpretation is further limited because of the [work's] saturation by the semantic and formal features of its matrix . . . ."[14] The reader's linguistic compe-tence (and especially the Bible reader's expectation of intertextuality), guided by the author's textual indicators, brings a solution to the puzzle, although there can never be absolute certainty that the solution dis-covered is the one intended by the author. The text exists as we have it, "and the ungrammaticalities, however revealing they may be, how-ever hermeneutically indicative, are still an obstacle. . . ."[15] Riffaterre contends that reading is unstable and interpretation never final.

The inherent instability of any intertextual relationship remains in spite of the author's apparent guidelines, and might perpetuate linger-ing doubt about the Johannine allusions to the Song, which are based on textual evidence. In order to address this difficulty, my study of the literary connections is followed by discussion of the allusions' textual and thematic corroboration from the Song itself, and the social con-text within which the Fourth Evangelist alluded to the Song.

A literary investigation must address the language of the texts. It is not clear whether the Johannine community's experience of the Song was in Greek or Hebrew, although it is likely that the Scripture to which the Gospel writer referred was the Septuagint. This widely held theory is not without its complexities, but arguments are persuasive, especially in regard to the texts studied here.[16] There is a notable aural relationship between the key words in Jn 12 and 20 and the Septuagint text of the Song, and this aural dimension is, of course, largely lacking in the Masoretic Text. The visual and auditory similari-

ties between the Johannine Greek text and the LXX Song text contribute to their overall consistency of relationship, but are not in any
way essential to the working of the allusions themselves. There is no
indication that the allusions *depend* on aural cues.

It would be useful to confirm the setting in which the Johannine
community knew the Song and to verify its influence on that community as compared with other Jewish Christian communities. Such a
study is, however, outside the scope of this investigation. The Song
may have been recited at Passover in the first century C.E., as it was in
the later rabbinic period. The Johannine association of both the death
and resurrection of Jesus and his anointing at Bethany with Passover
(19:31, 42 and 12:1) would contribute to the association among these
texts and the Song.[17] It is, however, the allusive literary connections
that confirm the relationship and resolve the Johannine enigmas.

Notes

1   See, for example, J. N. Sanders, "Those Whom Jesus Loved [John XI,5]," *New Testament Studies* I [1954–55]: 39–41; R. E. Brown, *The Gospel According to John*, Anchor Bible Series 29A (New York: Doubleday, 1970): 449–455; or J. F. Coakley, "The Anointing at Bethany and the Priority of John," *Journal of Biblical Literature* 107/2 (1988): 249–252.

2   The Evangelist is a "literary" writer in the sense intended by Robert Alter's distinction between literary allusions that arise out of the necessity of the form of expression employed, and nonliterary allusions that are merely rhetorical embellishments. Alter says, "Nothing confirms the literary character of biblical narrative and biblical poetry more strikingly than their constant, resourceful, and necessary recourse to allusion" (*The World of Biblical Literature* [New York: HarperCollins, 1992], 107).

3   Michael Fishbane insists that the Gospels are not properly studied in an intertextual relationship with the Hebrew Bible because they proclaim that they have fulfilled the ancient Israelite *traditum*. He asserts, "The position of inner-biblical exegesis is unique among the foundational documents of the Western religious tradition: neither the Gospels nor Pauline writings on the one hand, nor the Quran on the other, are quite like it. . . . Theirs is an innovative *traditio*, continuous with the Hebrew Bible but decidedly something new, something not 'biblical' . . ." (*Biblical Interpretation in Ancient Israel* [New York: Oxford University Press, 1985], 10). Gail O'Day, however, disputes Fishbane's premise that the New Testament cannot be included as Scripture for purposes of inner-biblical exegesis ("Jeremiah 9:22–23 and 1 Corinthians 1:26–31: A Study in Intertextuality," *Journal of Biblical Literature* 109 [1990]: 259–267).

4   M. Riffaterre, *Semiotics of Poetry* (Bloomington, IN: Indiana University Press, 1978), 2. Riffaterre defines *displacing* as "when the sign shifts from one meaning to another, when one word 'stands for' another"; *distorting* as "when there is ambiguity, contradiction, or nonsense"; and *creating* as "when textual space serves as a principle of organization for making signs out of linguistic items that may not be meaningful otherwise."

5   Ibid., 6.

6   Ibid.,5. Daniel Boyarin considers Riffaterre's ungrammaticalities the equivalent of the rabbinical "bumps in the text" ("Inner Biblical Ambiguity, Intertextuality and the Dialectic of Midrash: the Waters of Marah," *Prooftexts* 10 [1990]: 44).

7   Riffaterre emphasizes that "the obstacle that threatens meaning when seen in isolation at first reading is also the key to the semiosis, the key to significance in the higher system, where the reader perceives it as part of a complex network" (*Semiotics of Poetry*, 6).

8 Ibid., 164–165.

9 Z. Ben-Porat, "The Poetics of Literary Allusion," *PTL: A Journal for Descriptive Poetics and Theory of Literature* 1 (1976): 107–108.

10 Z. Ben-Porat, "Forms of Intertextuality and the Reading of Poetry: Uri Zvi Greenberg's *Basha'ar*," *Prooftexts* 10 (1990): 257.

11 Z. Ben-Porat, "The Poetics of Literary Allusion," 108–109.

12 Ibid., 109.

13 Ibid., 116.

14 Riffaterre, *Semiotics of Poetry*, 165.

15 Ibid.

16 See E. D. Freed's study of eighteen direct quotations from Scripture in the Fourth Gospel. Freed concludes that there is a stronger case for the LXX than for the MT (*Old Testament Quotations in the Gospel of John* [Leiden: E. J. Brill, 1965], 126). A similar case is made in R. E. Brown, *The Gospel According to John*, CXXVIX-CXXXII; M. K. H. Peters, "Septuagint," in *Anchor Bible Dictionary*, vol. V, ed. D. N. Freedman [New York: Doubleday, 1992], 1102); E. Tov, "The Septuagint," in *Mikra: Text, Translation, Reading and Interpretation of the Hebrew Bible in Ancient Judaism and Early Christianity*, ed. M. J. Mulder (Philadelphia: Fortress Press, 1988, 163); and D. Moody Smith "The Use of the Old Testament in the New," in *The Use of the Old Testament in the New and other essays*, ed. J. M. Efird Durham, NC: Duke University Press, 1972, 7).

17 The Song of Songs is one of the *Megilloth,* the scrolls containing the five books of the Writings assigned to be read at Jewish feasts. The Song was read at Passover. There is considerable imprecision about liturgical practice and the use of Scripture in either the Christian or Jewish communities in the first century C. E. S. M. Schneiders, however, claims that "the Canticle was the scroll used for the paschal celebration among the Jews which would suggest its use for the Easter narrative" ("The Johannine Resurrection Narrative," [S.T.D. diss., Pontificia Universitas Gregoriana, 1975], 363).

Chapter 2

Allusions to the Song of Songs
in Jn 12:1–8

Interpretive problems associated with the Johannine anointing and resurrection appearance accounts have led to considerable critical uncertainty. This study not only explains what the enigmatic texts intend, but also offers insight into the intertextual layer that has not previously been perceived. The literary theories of Riffaterre and Ben-Porat suggest important possibilities for understanding these Fourth Gospel accounts. This investigation of the puzzling elements of the Johannine anointing at Bethany focuses on the suspicion that the enigmas mark allusions to the Song of Songs.

Jn 12: 1-8

Ὁ οὖν Ἰησοῦς πρὸ ἓξ ἡμερῶν τοῦ πάσχα ἦλθεν εἰς Βηθανία, ὅπου ἦν Λάζαρος, ὃν ἤγειρεν ἐκ νεκρῶν Ἰησοῦς. ²ἐποίησαν οὖν αὐτῷ δεῖπνον ἐκεῖ, καὶ ἡ Μάρθα διηκόνει, ὁ δὲ Λάζαρο εἷς ἦν ἐκ τῶν ἀνακειμένων σὺν αὐτῷ. ³ Ἡ οὖν Μαριὰμ λαβοῦσα λίτραν μύρου νάρδου πιστικῆς πολυτίμου ἤλειψεν τοὺς πόδας τοῦ Ἰησοῦ καὶ ἐξέμαξεν ταῖς θριξὶν αὐτῆς τοὺς πόδας αὐτοῦ· ἡ δὲ οἰκία ἐπληρώθη ἐκ τῆς ὀσμῆς τοῦ μύρου. ⁴λέγει δὲ Ἰούδας ὁ Ἰσκαριώτης εἷς [ἐκ] τῶν μαθητῶν αὐτοῦ, ὁ μέλλων αὐτὸν παραδιδόναι· ⁵διὰ τί τοῦτο τὸ μύρον οὐκ ἐπράθη τριακοσίων δηναρίων καὶ ἐδόθη πτωχοῖς ⁶εἶπεν δὲ τοῦτο οὐχ ὅτι περὶτῶν πτωχῶν ἔμελεν αὐτῷ, ἀλλ᾽ ὅτι κλέπτης ἦν καὶ τὸ γλωσσόκομον ἔχων τὰ βαλλόμενα ἐβάσταζεν. ⁷εἶπεν οὖν ὁ Ἰησοῦς· ἄφες αὐτήν, ἵνα εἰς τὴν ἡμέραν τοῦ ἐνταφιασμοῦ μου τηρήσῃ αὐτό· ⁸τοὺς πτωχοὺς γὰρ πάντοτε ἔχετε μεθ᾽ ἑαυτῶν, ἐμὲ δὲ οὐ πάντοτε ἔχετε.

¹Six days before Passover Jesus came to Bethany, where Lazarus was, whom Jesus had raised from the dead. ²They made a dinner for him there; Martha was serving and Lazarus was one of those reclining at table with him. ³Mary, taking a pound of extremely precious nard ointment, anointed Jesus' feet and wiped his feet with her hair. And the house was filled with the smell of the ointment. ⁴Judas Iscariot, one of his disciples (the one who was about to betray him), said, ⁵Why was this ointment not sold for three hundred denarii and [the money] given to the poor? ⁶He said this not because the poor were a concern to him, but because he was a thief and, holding the money bag, he would take the contents. ⁷Jesus said, Let her be, so that she may keep it for the day of my burial. ⁸For you always have the poor with you, but you do not always have me.

An account of the anointing of Jesus by a woman figures in all four Gospels, attesting to the story's considerable appeal in several early Christian communities.[1] Each of the versions provides details that suggest the different community priorities influencing the individual Gospel accounts. There is hesitant consensus among interpreters that one fundamental story underlies all four versions. There is little consensus on anything else: neither the origin of the narrative, or its possible historicity, nor the priority of one account over the others, nor the interdependence of the accounts, nor the identity of the anointer, who is often mistakenly understood to be Mary Magdalene. Contrary to the claims of some interpreters, Mary Magdalene is not the anointer in any canonical Gospel.[2] Although Mary of Bethany and Mary Magdalene share several traits, the Evangelist clearly differentiates between them. The Christian tradition has for centuries conflated Mary Magdalene and Mary of Bethany, or Mary Magdalene and the Lucan sinner woman (Lk 7:36-50), as though "female lover of Jesus" characters in the New Testament were archetypal figures represented by different exemplars rather than particular human women. This conflation can be attributed to trivialization of the witness of women disciples and discounting of the experience of individual women, rather than to narrative or redactional considerations.[3]

The Hebrew Scriptures profoundly influenced the formation of the Gospel narratives and convictions about the meaning of the Scriptures, as well as preferences for particular portions of Scripture fashioned each community's distinctive shaping of the details of the Christian story. Examination of the redaction history of the Johannine anointing account and attention to the specific traits that distinguish it from the other three accounts provides insight into the scriptural background influencing the Fourth Gospel community. The themes of the Song served the Johannine community's expression of its self-understanding. Analysis of the Johannine anointing demonstrates the allusive hermeneutic exhibited by its connection to the Song. Clues in the Song clarify those perplexing features of the Johannine anointing account that remain problematic in contemporary interpretation, especially Mary's use of her hair (ἐξέμαξεν ταῖς θριξὶν αὐτῆς τοὺς πόδας αὐτοῦ) and the ointment's smell filling the house (ἡ δὲ οἰκία ἐπληρώθη ἐκ τῆς ὀσμῆς τοῦ μύρου). These details do not figure in the Synoptic anointing accounts. The Johannine narrative differs from the Synoptics in several other specifics: in the Fourth Gospel, Jesus is in the home of close friends and the anointing woman is named and is caring for her own guest. The person who objects to the anointing is also named. But the most important difference in the versions is in the anointing event itself.

Since the means of understanding the Johannine anointing account is found in its allusions to the Song of Songs, this chapter focuses on key words and on the Song verses to which Jn 12:1-8 alludes. Specific verses from the Song attract our attention because of their remarkable lexical correspondence to the Johannine anointing account or their description of an activity or setting notably similar to that described in Jn 12. Because there is no reason to insist on a fixed form to demonstrate an allusive relationship, no attempt is made to impose a systematic parallel between the Song and Jn 12. In any case, the Song's stanzas were not necessarily recited in a fixed order.

Particular words in the Johannine text alert the reader because they are potential indicators of allusion. They are the markers that set off the process of evoking another text. The most obvious of these evocative words is the startling statement that Mary wiped the ointment on Jesus' feet with her hair. Such a deed is too unusual to pass unnoticed in this otherwise unremarkable narrative, and this semantic indirection must be suspected of signaling an allusion to another text. Once one allusion is substantiated, other potential indicators of allusion become noticeable. Discussion of the Johannine reference to hair leads to other allusion-laden elements. And although hair might seem like an "overloaded marker," too common to denote a particular intertextual association, biblical reference to human hair is in fact remarkably rare.

Hair

A number of interpreters have approached the complication of Mary of Bethany's unusual use of her hair. Using historical-critical techniques, none has succeeded in resolving with any degree of confidence the perplexing question of why Mary wiped the ointment with her hair, or why a respectable woman took down her hair in the presence of men in the first place.[4] Some modern exegetes have difficulty believing that Mary would take down her hair in public to do something she could have done better with a towel; they find the anointing of feet unknown in antiquity; or they suggest that Mary was trying to keep from spoiling the cushions and rugs with dripping ointment. The preposterousness of these interpretations of Mary's gesture underlines the importance of an alternate explanation for her use of her hair. Interpretations of Mary's behavior have ranged from calling it "utter nonsense" to presuming that the detail is the result of a redactor's faulty conflation of the Synoptic versions.[5] The Johannine text makes excellent sense, however, once the reader discerns the allusive connection with the Song. As we have seen, a writer's intentional simultaneous activation of two texts is characteristic of the narrative process. The reader privileges one context over others, removing the ambiguity by choosing one of the possible alternatives. Realistically, this usually means choosing the alternative that appeals to the reader. Biblical writers use the techniques of literary allusion at least as extensively as secular writers do, because the biblical stories are perceived as the continuous unfolding of God's participation in human history.[6] Interpretive decisions to disambiguate in favor of "mistake" or "nonsense" in Jn 12:3 rather than to connect it with an earlier biblical text that also speaks of ointment, smell, and a beloved's hair ignore the significance of Mary of Bethany's action. In biblical narrative the memory of past experience always informs and enriches the present, although the signals of textual relationship may become, in Robert Alter's words, "microscopic."[7]

In Jn 12:3, Mary's use of her hair is an ungrammaticality, an expression that creates a semantic gap and threatens the reader's grasp of the reality (or mimesis) that the text describes. In the course of an otherwise logical narrative, the Evangelist describes an event that threatens verisimilitude. Mary uses her hair to wipe the ointment she has just applied to Jesus' feet. The puzzled reader is brought up short, but taking the text seriously as it stands and assuming a purpose on the author's part, the reader must look outside this text for a referent that will convey better sense to it. The question is where to look. The reader's ordinary literary competence makes possible the search for a referent text. In a biblical context one will naturally have a considerably heightened awareness of the probability that the present narrative is connected to an earlier one. Recognition of the theme will establish the link, for the biblical reader expects frequent intertextual connections.

Mary's use of her hair is an example of a *subtext*, in Riffaterre's scheme, a minor event with a significant hermeneutic function within the entire larger text. The insignificance of the event within the whole frees it to assume an "enormous ad hoc, context-dictated significance."[8] Because of the idiosyncratic nature of the subtext it is difficult to understand it without connecting it to some similar event. Therefore, Riffaterre insists, it works like memory built into the narrative. The search for the referent text and the search for the content of the memory, both lead the reader into the "unconscious" of the narrative where the allusion stands for memory.[9] The question for the reader is how to make the allusive connection, how to *identify* the evoked text. This process is not especially arcane, since one's facility with earlier texts of the same genre (in this case, Scripture) suggests associations. Alerted by the presence of a marker or ungrammaticality that hints at an allusion, one is likely to recognize other allusions.[10]

In the anointing stories of Matthew or Mark, in contrast to the Fourth Gospel account, there is no mention of hair. The Lucan woman, for whom it was perhaps appropriate to take down her hair in her publicly "sinful" circumstances, used her hair to dry the tears that had fallen on Jesus' feet as she wept penitently. Then she anointed his feet with ointment. Mary of Bethany did not weep and her motivation for anointing and wiping Jesus' feet is not articulated in the text. Reference to hair is unusual in Scripture. The only mention of human hair in the New Testament, outside of Jn 12 and its Lucan parallel, is in a small handful of parabolic texts in Matthew and Luke (Mt 5:36, 10:30; Lk 12:7, 21:18), in several admonitions about women's hairstyles in the Epistles (1 Cor 11:14-15; 1 Tim 2:9; 1 Pet 3:3), and in two physical descriptions in Revelation (Rev 1:14; 9:8). In the Old Testament outside of Leviticus, there is scant mention of human hair. There are, however, five specific references to hair in the Song of Songs.[11] In SS 4:1 and 6:5, the man compares his beloved's hair to a flock of goats streaming down a mountain. In SS 5:11, the woman describes her lover's flowing black locks. And in SS 7:6, there is a reference to hair, where the man tells the woman, "your head upon you is like Carmel, your flowing locks like purple, a king is bound in the tresses" (בִּרְהָטִים מֶלֶךְ אָסוּר/βασιλεὺς δεδεμένος ἐν παραδρομαῖς). The unusual mention of the woman's flowing hair in SS 7:6 and Mary of Bethany's apparently unbound hair in Jn 12:3, in both cases with the king as the object of the hair's "action," suggests an allusive link between the texts. The additional detail that the king is bound in the woman's hair (which is presumably still attached to her head) must surely be taken metaphorically and suggests the same physical immediacy as Mary's wiping Jesus' feet with her hair. The image does not seem to suggest that the king is literally tied up with the woman's hair. In the Fourth Gospel, the king is literally bound (δεδέμονος) in Jn 18:12 and 18:24. In the LXX, the Greek verbal connection is notable as well in SS 1:13, where the beloved is a "bundle of myrrh," that is, ἀπόδεσμος τῆς στακτῆς, between his lover's breasts. The MT refers instead to a small sack or pouch of myrrh (עְדֹור) between her breasts.

King, Reclining

The setting of the Johannine anointing story is the home of a character the reader knows to be an intimate friend of Jesus, Lazarus, whom Jesus had raised from the dead. This detail may imply that celebration and gratitude lie behind the Bethany family's preparation of a dinner in Jesus' honor (ἐποίησαν οὖν αὐτῷ δεῖπνον ἐκεῖ). It may also imply that the Lazarus-raising story and the anointing were not always told together, or were not always next to each other in the text. While Martha serves, Lazarus is reported to be one of those reclining at table with Jesus (ἀνακειμένων σὺν αὐτῷ). In SS 1:12, the king, whose title is an affectionate name for the beloved, is reclining at table (עַד־שֶׁהַמֶּלֶךְ בִּמְסִבּוֹ/ἕως οὗ ὁ βασιλεὺς ἐν ἀνακλίσει αὐτου). The Evangelist's interest in portraying Jesus as a king is evident from the first specific mention of this title in Jn 1:49 to the encounter between Jesus and Pilate in Jn 18:33-19:22 (see also Jn 6:15, 12:13, 12:15).[12] In an ironic exchange, Pilate asks Jesus if he is a king and then ridicules Jesus' kingship.[13] In Jn 19:14, Pilate announces to the crowds, "look, here is your king."[14]

Extremely Precious Nard Ointment

As the focal point of the anointing narrative, Jn 12:3 is also its central allusive link to the Song. By means of *allusion* the writer defines the anointing event as a reenactment of aspects of the Song. Detection of the link depends on the reader's ordinary linguistic ability to interpret, to notice which parts of the text do or do not make sense, and to compare this text to other possibly related texts.[15] Recognition of the link also depends on the presumption that the reader (or hearer) of the Fourth Gospel shares with the writer an expectation that the present text in some way continues an ancient tradition.[16] The Johannine text tells us that Mary of Bethany took a large quantity of μύρου νάρδου πιστικῆς πολυτίμου and anointed Jesus' feet.[17] The adjective πιστικῆς in the description of the ointment does not appear in the New Testament except in this account and its Marcan parallel and there is no consensus about the term's derivation. However this precise wording originated, it may have become part of the telling in the same way that such peculiarities are honored in folk and fairy tales, where the loose structure of the retelling often contains inexplicably precise wordings that must not vary because "the story is always told this way" (children are particularly insistent on such verbal precision). Historical criticism in biblical scholarship may exaggerate the need to explain the sources of such expressions. However, there is also the intriguing suggestion that πιστικῆς may be a corruption of τῆς στάκῆς, an oil from the storax shrub.[18] In view of the rarity of the expression, it is remarkable that in SS 1:12 the king-beloved is described as τῆς στάκῆς spending the night between the breasts of his lover.[19] The many allusions to the Song in Jn 12:1-3 suggest that the coincidence of the unusual words τῆς στάκῆς and πιστικῆς be taken seriously.

The appearance of the unique expression μύρου νάρδου πιστικῆς πολυτίμου in both the Johannine and Marcan versions of the anointing story has caused speculation that, in spite of the consensus that the Johannine account is independent of the others, such a curious verbal correspondence would ordinarily indicate a common oral or literary source.[20] The other evidence of allusion to the Song in the Johannine account suggests that the use of the πιστικῆς term for the ointment is intended to serve as a sign referring to the Song's τῆς στάκῆς and continues the formation of the intertextual patterns that the Evangelist aims to generate.

Feet

Mary's physical position is not stated in Jn 12:3, but the impression is that she is seated near Jesus' feet as he reclines, a position that fits her deed. This assumption goes beyond the textual evidence, and may suggest the Lucan Mary of Bethany. The fact that Martha is presented as "serving" in Jn 12:2, as she does in Lk 10:38-42, invites the impression that Mary is sitting at Jesus' feet, as in the Lucan text.[21] In SS 2:3, the Shulamite says, "I wanted to be in his shadow and I sat down" (בְּצִלּוֹ חִמַּדְתִּי וְיָשַׁבְתִּי/ἐν τῇ σκιᾷ αὐτοῦ ἐπεθύμησα καὶ ἐκάθισα). The fact that Mary anointed Jesus' feet rather than his head is noted in most exegetical studies.[22] Interpreters have varied opinions about the significance of this difference from the anointing of the head in Mark and Matthew's account, where it is likely that Jesus is symbolically shown to be king and messiah. Although Luke shares with the Fourth Gospel the anointing of feet, the Lucan "sinner in the city" has, we are told, different motivation from Mary's for anointing Jesus. The Lucan woman's gesture is presented as one of sorrow and repentance for her sinful past, as well as love (Lk 7:47-48). In addition, the Lucan account is chronologically unassociated with the time of Jesus' impending death and is the only anointing account of the four in which Jesus' burial is not mentioned. Mary's anointing may be intended as preparation for burial, as 12:7 indicates, or it may be a lavish sign of hospitality for the one the Fourth Evangelist portrays as king.

Can any hint can be found in the Song that might illuminate the reference to feet in Jn 12:3, or indicate a link between that text and the Song? In spite of the Song's abundant mention of ointment, perfume, and smell, no actual anointing is described. One must attend consciously to the fluidity of the poems that make up the Song, a fluidity that has been mentioned earlier in regard to their order, but which must also be emphasized in regard to their motifs. The lovers in the Song make beautiful, metaphorical observations about each other that are almost interchangeable from one lover to the other. They do not describe facts so much as create lovely pictures. Each lover's individual actions could as well be carried out by the other and textual hints need not be limited to descriptions of the specific behavior of the man or the woman.

The Song's only references to feet occur in SS 5:3 and 7:2. In 5:3 the man, whose hair is wet with dew, knocks during the night to be let into the woman's room, and she questions whether she should get up to let him in. She has already taken off her clothes and washed her feet, which she does not want to soil again.[23] There is nothing unusual about the woman's actions (except perhaps that she hesitates, given the urgency of the other verses), but the fact that feet are mentioned provides another hint of connection. Verse 5:5 says that when the woman opened to her beloved, her hands and fingers dripped myrrh (וְיָדַי נָטְפוּ־מֹר וְאֶצְבְּעֹתַי מֹר/χεῖρές μου ἔσταξαν σμύρναν, δάκτυλοί μου σμύρναν πλήρη). It is not clear why the myrrh was on her fingers, except that she has just described washing her feet for bed; anointing her feet might be part of her cleansing practice. Although Mary of Bethany's fingers are not specifically mentioned, it is probable that she used them to spread the ointment on Jesus' feet and that they "dripped myrrh." SS 7:2 is the opening of a *wasf* describing the woman's beauty starting from her feet and moving up to her head.[24] The foot reference is more specifically a description of her feet in motion, "steps" or dancing feet (פְּעָמַיִךְ/διαβήματά σου).

Scent

The Song says it is while the king is reclining that his lover's ointment gives forth its fragrance, and in the Johannine narrative, the odor of Mary's perfume fills the house while Jesus the king-beloved is reclining.[25] The Bethany family's banquet for Jesus, as described by the Fourth Evangelist, will have been more modest than a royal dinner, but the scene seems arranged to reflect the honor given a king, especially in the details about anointing, expensive ointment, and its smell. In SS 1:3 the woman says to her beloved, "the smell of your perfumes is above all spices" (לְרֵיחַ שְׁמָנֶיךָ טוֹבִים שֶׁמֶן/ὀσμὴ μύρων σου ὑπὲρ πάντα τὰ ἀρώματα). Her beloved, after whom young women run because of his scent (1:4), is said to be a king. As I note below in regard to גַּן/κῆπος, the Song's nine references to רֵיחַ/ὀσμὴ are a significant percentage of the entire biblical use of the word. There are thirty-one references in the Song to smell or perfume or their adjectival forms. Pleasant aroma is clearly of great worth in the Song, symbolizing more than the obvious delight it offers. The honor shown Jesus by Mary's anointing indicates that he is treated as a king.

The reference to the house being filled with the pervasive aroma of the perfume (12:3c), unique to the Fourth Gospel, draws attention to the detail of the smell. Its overtly symbolic aspect has been noted by many commentators, including Origen.[26] Since significant details in the Johannine anointing account arise from the Song of Songs matrix, the several occurrences of רֵיחַ/ὀσμὴ in the Song in which the smell is described as poured out or given forth heighten the intertextual relationship.

In SS 1:3, the woman says that the smell of her lover's ointments is better than all spices, that his name is ointment poured out (שֶׁמֶן תּוּרַק שְׁמֶךָ/ μύρον ἐκκενωθὲν ὄνομά σου).[27] SS 1:12 is suggestive of Jesus at table in Bethany. The Greek text, as Origen saw, ascribes the odor of the perfume to the beloved rather than to the nard itself: νάρδος μου ἔδωκεν ὀσμὴν αὐτοῦ. In addition, SS 2:13 refers to the vineyards blossoming, giving forth a smell (הַגְּפָנִים סְמָדַר נָתְנוּ רֵיחַ/αἱ ἄμπελοι κυπρίζουσιν, ἔδωκαν ὀσμήν). In SS 4:10-11, the bridegroom describes his bride's loving as "better than wine." The fragrance of her oils is better than balsam oils and the smell of her clothing is like the smell of Lebanon. In the Fourth Gospel, Jesus is symbolically understood as a bridegroom: he is referred to as the "bridegroom" by John the Baptist in Jn 3:29, replenishes the marriage wine at Cana in Jn 2:1-12, and is the bridegroom-at-the-well in the type-scene in Jn 4:1-42.[28]

The actualization of the original allusion, set in motion by the ungrammaticality of Mary's use of her hair, forms the basis for the intertextual patterning through which the Johannine text evokes the entire Song of Songs. This is a *metonymic* allusion that engages an element from an evoked text with the intent of bringing the entire evoked text to the reader's consciousness so that the two entire texts are experienced in relationship. In contrast, a metaphoric allusion remains specific to the single element it evokes in the referent text and does not intend to engage the whole text or to imply that the alluding and evoked texts share a larger connection. The earlier text (the Song) is reassessed because it is perceived in relation to the later text.[29] The effect of recognition of the Jn 12:3 allusions to the Song is a change in the reader's perception of the Johannine text as a whole. The reader's new comprehension of the textual relationship is largely based on common vocabulary within a wide context of fluid, transparent connections generated by the ungrammaticality. There is also a mystical motif to the perfume, a motif that depends on the widespread references in the Song to *house*, *aroma* and the overpowering *fullness* of perfume and smell, more than can be assimilated by the physical senses alone. In the context of the profoundly intimate encounter with Jesus which the Johannine community valued, Mary of Bethany's experience of Jesus' presence in the Bethany house could not be contained either within the space of the room or within her own sensory or spiritual perception. The reader, too, is overwhelmed by the impression of the nard's fragrance rising from Jesus' feet, perhaps his clothing, Mary's hands and hair, perhaps her clothing too. The perfume's most obvious symbolic referent is the Lord himself, whose presence fills and overflows the space like the very air (רוּחַ/πνεῦμα) on which the perfume's aroma is carried.

Notes

1   Aside from the Passion and Resurrection accounts, the anointing story shares this distinction only with the story of the feeding of the multitudes (the baptism of Jesus, narrated in the Synoptics, is not directly recounted in the Fourth Gospel, although it could be inferred from 1:32–33). The other anointing accounts are in Mark 14:3–9, Matthew 26:6–13, and Luke 7:36–50. The narrative details of the Lucan account differ from the those of the Johannine, as does its theological intention, but the two are often confused. K. E. Corley's study focuses on the Synoptic versions of Jesus' anointing at a meal (*Private Women, Public Meals* [Peabody, MA: Hendrickson Publishers, Inc., 1993], esp. 102–106, 121–130, 169–172).

2   For one summary of opinion on the woman's identity and the number of anointings, see A. Feuillet, "Les deux onctions faites sur Jésus, et Marie-Madeleine," *Revue Thomiste* 75 (1975): 353–394.

3   Disparagement of women's experience is borne out by the often absurd explanations offered for Mary of Bethany's wiping Jesus' feet with her hair. S. M. Schneiders recognizes the discounting of Christian women's authority in, for example, "Women in the Fourth Gospel and the Role of Women in the Contemporary Church," *Biblical Theology Bulletin* 12 (1982): 35–45.

4   Public exposure of a woman's hair is specifically censured in 1 Cor. 11:5–16, a pre-Johannine text. J. Jeremias says that "it was the greatest disgrace for a woman to unbind her hair in the presence of men," and he quotes supporting rabbinic sources (*The Parables of Jesus* [London: SCM Press, 1963], 126). Referring to Mary's use of her hair, J. E. Bruns contends that "obviously the story had a firm place in the primitive oral gospel, but only form criticism can hope to restore its original content" ("A Note on Jn 12,3," *Catholic Biblical Quarterly*, 28 (1966): 220). Little further clarity on the issue of Mary's hair has ensued in the thirty years since Bruns' article, form-criticism notwithstanding. In discussion of the Song of Songs, Ariel Bloch and Chana Bloch note that "in ancient Mesopotamian society, it was improper for a woman, especially one of the higher classes, to bare her head in public; conversely, a common harlot had to keep her head uncovered, and was not permitted to veil herself like other women" (*The Song of Songs: A New Translation* [New York: Random House, 1995], 167).

5   J. F. Coakley summarizes scholarship in "The Anointing at Bethany and the Priority of John," 241–256. See also C.H. Giblin, "Mary's Anointing for Jesus' Burial-Resurrection (John 12,1–8)," *Biblica* 73 (1992): 560–564.

6   In his discussion of midrash, D. Boyarin stresses the function of *ambiguity* as a textual stimulus impelling the reader to make a connection with another text. He cites L. Patterson's observation that "a text is ambiguous only to someone" and that "disambiguating is always . . . a process of deciding not

what a text means but what we want it to mean" (*Negotiating the Past* [Madison: University of Wisconsin Press, 1987], 150–151).

7   Alter asserts that "as signals in the allusive marker become more microscopic, the dimension of teasing game may become more prominent. . . . [the marker] may function as a subliminal clue, affecting the perception of the story in ways which are not conscious; and in general it is likely that a good deal of allusion is either meant to have or ends up having a subliminal effect" (*The Pleasures of Reading* [New York: Simon and Schuster, 1989], 121). The "teasing game" seems especially appropriate to the Song of Songs context.

8   M. Riffaterre, *Fictional Truth* (Baltimore: The Johns Hopkins University Press, 1990), 59. Riffaterre explains further that "in the narrative, the subtext connects its own topic or its minidrama metonymically, metaphorically, or symbolically with one of the [story's] sequences of events or even with the main sequence, and with the telos of each."

9   Ibid., 100.

10   According to Ben-Porat, the perception of one allusion makes one alert to the presence of subsequent allusions, which compounds the allusive effect, suggests further, undetected, allusions, and prevents one from ignoring these markers ("Forms of Intertextuality and the Reading of Poetry," 270).

11   M. Falk would include another, noting that (תֹּרִים/τρυγόνες) of SS 1:10 appropriately refers to the woman's *braids* (*The Song of Songs* [San Francisco: HarperCollins, 1990], 171). In addition, Bloch and Bloch also claim a second reference to hair at 4:1, and they believe that 4:3 refers to hair, as does 6:7.

12   J. E. Bruns states that "the interest of the fourth evangelist in the royalty of Jesus is apparent. It is not so much the occasional reference to kingship (1,49; 6,15; 12,13–15; 18,33–19,3; 19,13–22) as the total picture of Jesus as the glorified Son of Man whose lifting-up (on the Cross: 3,14; 12,32) is a real enthronement" ("A Note on Jn 12,3," 219). R. J. Cassidy says, "The concept of Jesus' kingship continues as a significant element within the larger portrayal of Jesus' sovereignty that John provides . . ." (*John's Gospel in New Perspective* (Maryknoll, NY: Orbis Books, 1992), 50). In regard to "John's overall portrayal of Jesus' kingly identity" Cassidy says, "this topic presumably held more than minimal interest to John's readers throughout the Roman empire."

13   The function of irony in the Fourth Gospel is the subject of a number of important studies, including those of R. A. Culpepper, *The Anatomy of the Fourth Gospel* (Philadelphia: Fortress Press, 1983); Paul Duke, *Irony in the Fourth Gospel* (Atlanta: John Knox Press, 1985); and Gail R. O'Day, *Revelation in the Fourth Gospel* (Philadelphia: Fortress Press, 1986). O'Day claims that the literary technique of irony is the most important vehicle of revelation in the Gospel and that ironic presentations must therefore be suspected of bearing important Johannine theology. O'Day emphasizes that the narrative itself is the mode of revelation in the Fourth Gospel (ibid., 33–48).

14   J. K. Elliott affirms that "the original core of the story of Jesus' anointing therefore tells of his consecration as king and thus the story is clearly connected with the story of the triumphal entry, in which Jesus is hailed as King-Messiah [Jn 12:12f]" ("The Anointing of Jesus," *The Expository Times* 85 [1974]: 106). J. N. Sanders is of the same opinion ("Those Whom Jesus Loved," 37).

15   In Riffaterre's terms, the "heuristic" reading is where interpretation first takes place and meaning is first apprehended. The reader assumes that language is referential and that incompatibilities are perceptable. The reader's identification of expressions that are not literally logical (such as tropes and figures of speech) makes a "semantic transfer" possible (*Semiotics of Poetry*, 5).

16   Referring to the Hebrew Bible, Robert Alter asserts that ". . . the matrix for allusion is often a sense of absolute historical continuity and recurrence, or an assumption that earlier events and figures are timeless ideological models by which all that follows can be measured" (*The World of Biblical Literature*, 117).

17   A. Legault claims that the anointing of feet was unknown in the period ("An Application of the Form-Critique Method to the Anointings in Galilee (Lk 7:36-50), and Bethany (Mt 26:6-13, Mk 14:3-9, Jn 12:1-8)," *Catholic Biblical Quarterly* 16 [1954]: 137-138. R. E. Brown finds such anointing "unparalleled," but reconciles it theologically by claiming that the Fourth Evangelist intended to symbolize the preparation for Jesus' burial (*Gospel According to John*, 454). J. F. Coakley, however, supplies a catalogue of instances of the anointing of feet in antiquity and concludes that although such anointing would have been highly unusual, "it could be a natural and spontaneous act of extravagance in any society that set store by the use of oils and perfumes" ("The Anointing at Bethany and the Priority of John," 248).

18   See Brown, *Gospel According to John*, 448. Brown does not specify whether the "corruption" is textual or simply a modification in the language. He does not suggest a connection between Jn 12:3 and the Song, nor does he mention the possible coincidence of wording. Bruns refers to P. L. Couchoud's suggestion that πιστικῆς is a corrupt reading of τῆς στάκῆς and that "the use of this phrase depends upon a passage in Polybius relating to the eccentricities of Antiochus Epiphanes" which he cites ("A Note on John 12,3," 220-221).

19   As in the case of SS 1:12, where it is not clear in the Hebrew text whether the king's or the nard's fragrance is given forth, here it is ambiguous whether the beloved or the bundle of myrrh spends the night between the lover's breasts. The Greek verb αὐλίζομαι strongly suggests a human subject, but the Hebrew ין לִ in the MT does not necessarily so imply. See the "Notes Complémentaires" on Origen's *Commentaire sur le Cantique des Cantiques*, Tome II, Sources Chrétiennes 376, L. Brésard and H. Crouzel (Paris: Éditions du Cerf, 1992), 773, where it is maintained that the parallelism basic to He-

brew poetry demands that the beloved be identified with the perfume in SS 1:12.

20 Coakley suggests that the likelihood of the preservation of the expression μύρου νάρδου πιστικῆς πολυτίμου would be enhanced if it were the proper name of a particular kind of ointment ("The Anointing at Bethany," 241). In contrast to other interpreters, he argues for the priority of the histori-cal tradition underlying the Fourth Gospel account. Although most scholars argue that the names of the characters in the Johannine account are an addi-tion that axiomatically indicates the secondary, late status of that version, such naming might rather indicate a different focus or goal in telling the story. Moreover, Coakley suggests that the fact that Mary of Bethany is identified in Jn 11:2 as "the one who anointed the Lord with perfume and wiped his feet with her hair" may mean that the tradition identified her specifically with that action (ibid., 245).

21 See Martin Scott's discussion of Martha's "serving" role in Sophia and the Johannine Jesus (Sheffield: JSOT Press, 1992), 212-214. On Mary's physi-cal position, see also Benages, "La Fragrancia del Perfume," 247.

22 See Coakley, "The Anointing at Bethany,"; D. Daube, "The Anointing at Bethany and Jesus' Burial," Anglican Theological Review 32 (1950): 186-199; Elliott, "The Anointing of Jesus,"; Feuillet, "Les deux onctions faites sur Jésus,"; E. R. Goodenough, "John, a Primitive Gospel," Journal of Bib-lical Literature 64 (1945): 145–182; R. Holst, "The One Anointing of Jesus: another Application of the Form-Critical Method," Journal of Biblical Lit-erature 95 (1976): 435–446; M.-J. Lagrange, "Jésus a-t-il été oint plusieurs fois et par plusieurs femmes?" Revue Biblique 9 (1912): 504–532; Legault, "An Application of the Form-Critique Method"; B. Prete, "Un' Aporia giovannea: il testo di Giov. 12,3," Rivista Biblica Italiana 25 (1977): 357–374; J. N. Sanders, "Those Whom Jesus Loved (John XI,5)," 29–41.

23 The reference to removing garments and washing feet suggests the relation-ship between the Johannine anointing at Bethany and the foot-washing in Jn 13. Mary of Bethany's action in chapter 12 foretells and parallels Jesus' wash-ing of the disciples' feet in chapter 13. Mary takes the role Jesus will have in chapter 13, and Jesus the role that Peter at first refuses (Jn 13:6). Jesus removed some of his clothes before washing his friends' feet, and Mary's taking down her hair would have been the cultural equivalent of taking off her clothes under the circumstances.

The theological issues underscored in both the Johannine anointing and foot-washing narratives are similar and are those valued in the Song. M. Scott has detailed some of the resemblances between Jn 12:1–8 and Jn 13:1–20, focusing on the theology of true discipleship central to each account, and concluding that "the parallel between Mary's action and that of Jesus toward the μαθηταὶ in 13.1–20 is unmistakable" (Sophia and the Johannine Jesus, 211).

24   The *wasf* is an Arabic poetic form in which the beloved's (male or female) body is extolled through a systematic description of its beauty from head to toe or from toe to head. *Wasfs* are found in chapters 4, 5, and 7 of the Song of Songs.

25   Michel Cambe also agrees that the Evangelist intended to evoke SS 1:12. Cambe cites Esther 2:12, a description of the custom among Near-Eastern women of using lavish amounts of perfume, and he proposes that the young woman in the Song might be following the practice of anointing important guests at a banquet with perfume. He suggests other similarities between SS 1:12 and Jn 12:3: during a banquet a woman dispenses a profuse amount of nard in honor of a king and the nard's odor is penetrating ("L'influence du Cantique des Cantiques sur le Nouveau Testament," *Revue Thomiste* 62 (1962): 16).

26   Cambe emphasizes the extraordinary opulence of the Johannine anointing account and cites the profusion of perfume, the exceptional anointing of feet, and the house filled with the nard's fragrance. Emphasizing the rare word ὀσμή, he believes the Evangelist intended to indicate the relationship to the Song ("L'influence du Cantique," 15–17).

       N. C. Benages concludes that the perfume's fragrance symbolizes Christ's victory over death. She determines that the statement "the house was filled with the smell of the ointment" is inspired by the Song of Songs and by Pauline doctrine. She understands the odor in much the same way as Origen did, that it is the odor of Christ which the nard absorbs and then gives forth ("La Fragrancia del Perfume en Jn 12,3," *Estudios Biblicos* 48 [1990]: 243–265).

       R. E. Brown suggests that the detail of the smell filling the house parallels the Marcan reference to the anointing woman's deed being made known throughout the whole world (Mk 14:9). He bases this assessment on the rabbinic Midrash Rabbah on Qoheleth 7:1. Brown notes that "if this rabbinic comparison was known at the time when the Fourth Gospel was written, then there is indeed a parallel between the Marcan and Johannine ideas" (*Gospel According to John*, 453).

       In spite of his certainty about the Song's relation to Jn 20:11–18, A. T. Hanson understands Haggai 2:6-9 to underlie Jn 12:1–8. Hanson insists that the unique Johannine reference to the smell of the nard filling the house "echoes Scripture more decidedly than any other" verse in 12:1–8, but he believes it is intended to evoke Haggai 6:7 (*The New Testament Interpretation of Scripture* [London: SPCK, 1980], 119). See also *The Prophetic Gospel* (Edinburgh: T&T Clark, 1991), 163. Although Hanson mounts a creditable argument for the relationship with Haggai, his premise rests on an intricate weaving of scriptural references that bypasses the simpler, more patent details of the Johannine account which are better taken at face value. Hanson does not mention the detail of Mary's hair, which has been an important stumbling block in interpretation.

27   Brown notes the similarity between SS 1:3 and Qoh 7:1, which he quotes in
     regard to the possible parallel between Jn 12:3c and Mk 14:9.

28   Referring to Abraham's servant and Rebekah at the well (Gen. 24:1–67), R.
     Alter asserts that the "most striking feature of this version of the type-scene is
     its slow, stately progress, an effect achieved by the extensive use of dialogue,
     by a specification of detail clearly beyond the norm of biblical narrative, and,
     above all, by a very elaborate use of the device of verbatim repetition, which
     is a standard resource of the biblical writers" (*The Art of Biblical Narrative*.
     [New York: Basic Books, 1981], 53). S. M. Schneiders discusses the increas-
     ing importance of marital symbolism in the Old Testament and its use in the
     Fourth Gospel ("The Johannine Resurrection Narrative," 355–361).

29   The favored Christian practice of interpreting the Song allegorically as a de-
     scription of the relation of Jesus and the individual believer may have been
     influenced by more than a similar Jewish allegorical tradition. The basis for
     the Christian allegory is strengthened by the Johannine allusion's effect on
     the Song, which causes the Song itself to be understood in a new context.

Chapter 3

Allusions to the Song of Songs in Jn 20: 1, 11–18

Many clues encourage recognition of the intertextual relationship between Jn 12:1–8 and the Song of Songs. The plentiful allusions not only deepen the Johannine text's significance, but also attest to the hermeneutic connections between the Fourth Gospel and the Song. Problematic textual areas in Jn 20:1,11–18 are also resolved through investigation of their connection with the Song. Just as details in the Johannine anointing account often baffle readers and lead them to question the narrative itself, questions about the Johannine resurrection appearance account move readers to consider whether this text too is intended to evoke another text. Again the evidence points toward allusions to the Song of Songs. Study of key words offers clues to the meaning of the puzzling portions of the story. Just as in the anointing account, several instances of semantic indirection in Jn 20:11–18 influence readers to suspect that they do not understand the story and to ask whether it may refer to something outside itself. Jn 20:1 is the appropriate narrative introduction to the Magdalene story continued in verses 11–18, and text criticism suggests that Jn 20:1–18 may combine several oral fragments.[1] A focus is on the intimate relationship between two friends as mirrored in the Song of Songs limits discussion to the Johannine textual unit that tells that story.

Jn 20: 1,11–18

¹Τῇ δὲ μιᾷ τῶν σαββάτων Μαρία ἡ Μαγδαληνὴ ἔρχεται πρωὶ σκοτίας ἔτι οὔσης εἰς τὸ μνημεῖον καὶ βλέπει τὸν λίθον ἠρμένον ἐκ τοῦ μνημείου. ¹¹Μαρία δὲ εἰστήκει πρὸς τῷ μνημείῳ ἔξω κλαίουσα. ὡς οὖν ἔκλαιεν, παρέκυψεν εἰς

τὸ μνημεῖον ¹²καὶ θεωρεῖ δύο ἀγγέλους ἐν λευκοῖς
καθεζομένους, ἕνα πρὸς τῇ κεφαλῇ καὶ ἕνα πρὸς τοῖς
ποσίν, ὅπου ἔκειτο τὸ σῶμα τοῦ Ἰησοῦ. ¹³καὶ λέγουσιν
αὐτῇ ἐκεῖνοι· γύναι, τί κλαίεις; λέγει αὐτοῖς ὅτι ἦραν τὸν
κύριον μου, καὶ οὐκ οἶδα ποῦ ἔθηκαν αὐτόν. ταῦτα εἰποῦσα
ἐστράφη εἰς τὰ ὀπίσω καὶ θεωρεῖ τὸν' Ἰησοῦν ἑστῶτα καὶ
οὐκ ᾔδει ὅτι Ἰησοῦς ἐστιν. ¹⁵λέγει αὐτῇ Ἰησοῦς· γύναι, τί
κλαίεις; τίνα ζητεῖς; ἐκείνη δοκοῦσα ὅτι ὁ κηπουρός ἐστιν
λέγει αὐτῷ· κύριε, εἰ σὺ ἐβάστασας αὐτόν, εἰπέ μοι ποῦ
ἔθηκας αὐτόν, καγὼ αὐτὸν ἀρῶ. ¹⁶λέγει αὐτῇ Ἰησοῦς· Μαριάμ.
στραφεῖσα ἐκείνη λέγει αὐτῷ Ἑβραϊστί· ῥαββουνι (ὃ λέγεται
διδάσκαλε). ¹⁷λέγει αὐτῇ Ἰησοῦς· μή μου ἅπτου, οὔπω γὰρ
ἀναβέβηκα πρὸς τὸν πατέρα· πορεύου δὲ πρὸς τοὺς ἀδελφούς
μου καὶ εἰπὲ αὐτοῖς· ἀναβαίνω πρὸς τὸν πατέρα μου καὶ
πατέρα ὑμῶν καὶ θεόν μου καὶ θεὸν ὑμῶν. ¹⁸ἔρχεται Μαριὰμ
ἡ Μαγδαληνὴ ἀγγέλλουσα τοῖς μαθηταῖς ὅτι ἑώρακα τὸν
κύριον, καὶ ταῦτα εἶπεν αὐτῇ.

¹On the first day of the week, early, while it was still dark, Mary
Magdalene came to the tomb, and she saw the stone removed from
the tomb. ¹¹But Mary stood outside the tomb crying. As she was
crying, she peeked into the tomb,¹² and she saw two angels in white
sitting, one at the head and one at the feet where the body of
Jesus had been lying. ¹³They said to her, "Woman, why are you
crying?" She said to them, "They took away my Lord, and I do not
know where they put him." ¹⁴Having said this, she turned around,
and she saw Jesus standing, but she did not know that it was Jesus.
¹⁵Jesus said to her, "Woman, why are you crying? Who are you
looking for?" Thinking that he was the gardener, she said to him,
"Sir, if you took him, tell me where you put him and I will take
him." ¹⁶Jesus said to her, "Mary." She, turning, said to him in
Hebrew, "Rabbouni" (which means Teacher). ¹⁷Jesus said to her,
"Do not hold me, for I have not yet ascended to the father. But go
to my sisters and brothers and tell them, I am ascending to my
father and your father, to my God and your God." ¹⁸Mary Magdalene
came and announced, "I have seen the Lord, and he told me these
things."

Like the anointing at Bethany, the Johannine account of Jesus'
resurrection appearance to Mary Magdalene uses literary allusion to
activate intertextual patterns with the Song of Songs.² Recognition of

the allusions in Jn 20 is also triggered by ungrammaticalities, albeit subtler and less easily identifiable examples than those seen in the anointing account.[3] Unrecognized allusive markers in the resurrection appearance account have put critical interpreters as well as ordinary readers in a quandary. The specific markers are references to Mary's "turning" in Jn 20:14 (ἐστράφη εἰς τὰ ὀπίσω) and 20:16 (στραφεῖσα) and Jesus' command to Mary in 20:17 not to hold him (μή μου ἅπτου). There are other allusions to the Song in the appearance account as well, but the allusions in vv. 14, 16, and 17 function as the "bumps in the text" that first seize the reader's attention. The repetition of στρέφω in 20:14 and 20:16 implies that Mary Magdalene is turning round and round. This image figures importantly in the intertextual pattern the Evangelist sets in motion. So too in 20:17, when Jesus tells Mary not to continue touching (or holding) him and the text does not indicate that she is touching him, the reader is drawn up short and impelled by the "bump" to look for a possible allusion.

A study of the markers (20:14, 16 and 20:17) whose apparent illogic alerts the reader to the possibility of involving another text leads to the suspicion that the Song of Songs is the evoked text. A focus on key words leads to other areas of the narrative of Jesus' appearance where motifs, vocabulary, or actions corroborate the intertextual pattern set in motion by ungrammaticalities. Enigmatic textual details in the Johannine narrative can be clarified by examining how the allusions simultaneously activate both the resurrection appearance and the Song. A literary focus differs from the theological focus characteristically brought to bear on this pericope, but investigation confirms and strengthens the conclusions reached in a theological frame of reference, while also providing insight into how the text itself works to develop theological symbolism. While the Mary Magdalene episode is central for the Fourth Gospel's theology, the contribution of the episode's literary intricacy to the formation of Johannine theology has been underestimated. Activation of the literary allusions to the Song and actualization of the subsequent intertextual patterns immeasurably deepen the reader's theological perception.

Turning

Perplexing markers that reveal allusions do not necessarily occur at the beginning of the narrative. On the contrary, one is likely to be moving satisfactorily through the story when an ungrammaticality abruptly calls into question all one has perceived to be happening so far. At this point one is compelled to reconsider the text from the beginning. During this *retroactive* or *hermeneutic* reading, Riffaterre says, the reader begins to compare backwards, reviewing and revising,

> in effect performing a structural decoding; as he moves through the text he comes to recognize, by dint of comparisons or simply because he is now able to put them together, that successive and differing statements, first noticed as mere ungrammaticalities, are in fact equivalent, for they now appear as variants of the same structural matrix.[4]

Riffaterre's description of the reader's "conversion" to a new understanding of the text parallels the Fourth Evangelist's description of the believer's conversion to a new perception of Jesus, especially—perhaps ironically—as it applies to the usual metaphorical interpretation of Mary's "turning" as Christian conversion.

The obstacle to meaning becomes the key to meaning once the reader perceives the invitation to consider another dimension, an intertextual dimension. The reader of the Johannine appearance narrative may be drawn into Mary's emotional state and share her confusion about the interior of Jesus' tomb and the identity of the man she encounters. She is presented as a woman looking desperately for someone she loves, and she is clearly distraught. The Fourth Gospel reader does not come to this text in a narrative vacuum, but is instead conscious that the Song has been a significant referent text elsewhere in the Gospel. The context of a woman's search for her beloved heightens the reader's perhaps subconscious mindfulness of the role the Song has played in the Gospel.

Since the reader reconsiders the episode's initial scene only after arriving at the inconsistency, the narrative is engaging and provocative but not puzzling until one comes to στρέφω. With or without an awareness of the theological *double entendre* in regard to στρέφω, one recognizes an incongruity. The ambiguity in the text must be reconciled by choosing an intertextual context to which it may relate.[5] Although στρέφω may be an "overloaded" marker with myriad possible referents, the astute reader is drawn to begin the disambiguating process by evoking a previously fruitful referent text, one already seen in relationship to another Johannine story about a woman named Mary.

When Mary Magdalene turns to speak to Jesus (20:14) and during their conversation, turns again (20:16), the "turnings" may be under-

stood at a metaphorical level to refer to Mary's spiritual conversion.[6]
But at the immediate narrative level they do not make sense and leave
a gap that invites a midrashic process of discernment. According to
Daniel Boyarin,

> the reader must fill in the gaps, forming hypotheses about what is left out of
> the text. . . . The gaps are those silences in the text which call for interpreta-
> tion if the reader is to 'make sense' of what happened, to fill out the plot and
> the characters in a meaningful way. . . .[7]

Boyarin defines a gap as any element in the biblical text that requires
interpretation in order to construct the story coherently, including not
only omitted elements, but also repetitions and contradictions. All of
these elements tell the reader that he or she must fill in something
missing so as to be able to read the text. A hermeneutic reading of the
Johannine episode begins by testing its connection to the Song. It is
immediately notable that in several places the Song contains references to words related to στρέφω. In SS 2:17 the woman says סֹב דּוֹדִי/
ἀπόστρεψον ἀδελφιδέ μου. In 6:5, the man says הָסֵבִּי עֵינַיִךְ מִנֶּגְדִּי/
ἀπόστρεψον ἀφθαλμούὅ σου ἀπεναντίον μου; in 7:1, the
chorus of daughters of Jerusalem calls out to the woman
שׁוּבִי שׁוּבִי הַשּׁוּלַמִּית שׁוּבִי שׁוּבִי וְנֶחֱזֶה־בָּךְ/ἐπίστρεφε ἐπίστρεφε ἡ
Σουλαμῖτις, ἐπίστρεφε ἐπίστρεφε, καὶ ὀψόμεθα ἐν σοι.[8] In
7:11, the woman says, אֲנִי לְדוֹדִי וְעָלַי תְּשׁוּקָתוֹ/'Εγὼ τῷ ἀδελφιδῷ
μου, καὶ ἐπ' ἐμὲ ἡ ἐπιστροφὴ αὐτοῦ. In addition, in verse 6:1,
the daughters of Jerusalem ask the woman, אָנָה הָלַךְ דּוֹדֵךְ אָנָה פָּנָה דוֹדֵךְ/
ποῦ ἀπέβλεψεν ὁ ἀδελφιδός σοῦ καὶ ζητήσομεν αὐτὸν μετὰ
σοῦ. The unusual number of words related to "turning" in the Song is
significant in interpreting its possible connection to Jn 20. While the
link may appear trifling or superficial by the typical historical-critical
criteria of relationship, the norms of literary intertextuality include
such highly elusive and oblique verbal echoes.[9] It is more than coinci-
dental that the call of the daughters of Jerusalem to the searching
woman, "Turn, turn" should apply so uncannily to Mary Magdalene,
the searching woman turning and turning.[10] As Boyarin maintains in
regard to midrashic interpretation, resolutions of the ambiguities presented in a text are choices made from interpretive options within
Scripture.[11] Referring to Riffaterre's "dual sign," Boyarin suggests that
textual awkwardness points semiotically to another text that provides
a solution.

Do Not Hold Me

One of the most discussed interpretive dilemmas in this resurrection appearance account is Jesus' charge to Mary that she not hold him (20:17) when there is no textual indication that she is holding him. A few manuscripts have the phrase that Mary ran forward to touch Jesus after she recognized him (καὶ προσέδραμεν ἅψασθαι αὐτοῦ, 20:16b), an addition perhaps designed to make better sense of Jesus' command whose rationale has not been told to the reader.[12] The present imperative μή μου ἅπτου implies that Mary is in the act of touching Jesus.[13] Since there is no such indication in the text, the phrase becomes another ungrammaticality that hints at the structure of the textual matrix. Jesus' unwarranted injunction raises a central topic of the appearance account even while it remains illogical. The apparently unreasonable command focuses in two related directions. Theologically, it raises the issue of Jesus' post-resurrection corporeality (and corporeality is surely integral to the Song), and literarily it marks the allusion.[14] A unique characteristic of allusion is that it is not limited to a description in the referent text, but it may also elicit the implications of the situation described in the evoked text without specifically quoting that text. Robert Alter asserts that

> allusion is pervasive in the Bible [because] this was, on the evidence of the texts themselves, a traditional culture that encouraged a high degree of verbatim retention of its own classical texts. . . . [A] revelation of a shift in attitude, perspective, or situation is introduced through the alteration of a single word, the deletion of a phrase, the addition of a word, a switch in the order of items, as statements are repeated; it is a technique with a power and subtlety that could have worked only on an audience accustomed to retain minute textual details as it listened and thus to recognize the small but crucial changes introduced in repetition.[15]

The Johannine listener would be likely to pick up verbal echoes and corresponding situations, such as the Mary Magdalene episode and the love song. At the same time, an evoked text (here, the Song) might be used simply for narrative purposes, "to underline a theme, define a motive or character, provide a certain orientation toward an event."[16] Although the Song does not literally say that the man told the woman not to hold him (on the contrary, in fact), the situation the Song describes is sufficiently like that of Jn 20:17 to include it in a discussion of rhetorical intertextuality.[17]

Jesus' command is comprehensible in terms of SS 3:4, in which the woman who finds her beloved says אֲחַזְתִּיו וְלֹא אַרְפֶּנּוּ/ἐκράτησα αὐτὸν καὶ οὐχ ἀφῆκα αὐτόν.[18] The Song's refrain, "I sought him whom my soul loves, but could not find him," also occurs in 3:1-2. The Johannine writer has drawn the reader to see a resemblance to the Song with its lover seeking her beloved and it does not require much imagination to see that the most likely immediate response of the woman to finding the beloved she seeks would be to embrace him.

Night

Jn 20:1 sets the scene for the narrative that is continued in verse 11. The emphasis is on Mary Magdalene's arrival at Jesus' tomb while it is still night (πρωῒ σκοτίας ἔτι οὔσης), a woman alone and apparently without anointing spices. The Johannine resurrection account is the only one of the four that specifies that Mary Magdalene was by herself. [19] It draws motifs from Song of Songs 3:1-4, verses which support the idea of a woman alone wandering about at night seeking one she deeply loves, whose disappearance consumes her attention. In SS 3:1, the woman seeking her beloved goes out בַּלֵּילוֹת/ἐν νυξὶν to find him, and in SS 5:2 the woman whose heart is awake hears her beloved knocking; he begs her to let him in because his hair is wet with the dew of night, רְסִיסֵי לָיְלָה/ψεκάδων νυκτός. The exceptional nature of such solitary nocturnal behavior on the part of a woman in ancient Palestine alerts one familiar with the Song to its relationship with this Johannine account. The fact that both the woman lover in the Song and Mary Magdalene have similar motives for their highly unusual conduct makes the texts' connection all the more plausible. Mary Magdalene's role remarkably parallels that of the Shulamite.[20]

Tomb

Twice in Jn 20:1 and twice again in 20:11, the narrator refers to τὸ μνημεῖον. The tomb is the sort a person can step into, a small room. In verse 1:4 of the Song, there is reference to another kind of small room, τὸ ταμίειον (MT הֶדֶר). In the LXX, SS 1:4 says, εἰσήνεγκέν με ὁ βασιλεὺς εἰς τὸ ταμίειον αὐτοῦ.[21] Twice more, in verses 3:4 and 8:2, the Song refers to τὸ ταμίειον;[22] in both cases, the woman wants to bring her lover into her mother's house, into the

ταμίειον of the one who conceived her.[23] The Song's five references
to the "mother," especially the two to "my mother's house," (the other
three references are in SS 1:6, 8:1, and 8:5) offer an engaging echo
with Jesus' saying to Mary Magdalene in verse 20:17 that he is going
to "the father," to "my father and your father" (see also Jesus' reference in Jn 14:2 to his father's house).

Garden

The Fourth Evangelist's unique report that Jesus' tomb was in a garden associates it with the garden setting in the Song (4:12,16; 5:1;
8:13). A considerable portion of the total number of scriptural references to garden are found in the Song. The Fourth Evangelist is alone
in setting Jesus' burial in a garden tomb (Jn 19:41).[24] When Mary
Magdalene turns and sees Jesus standing nearby, she mistakes him for
the gardener. In SS 4:12, the man calls his beloved גַּן נָעוּל מַעְיָן חָתוּם/
κῆπος κεκλεισμένος πηγὴ ἐσφραγισμένη. He adds שְׁלָחַיִךְ פַּרְדֵּס/
ἀποστολαίσου παράδεισος (4:13) preceding the list of spices in
her garden, which include נֵרְדְּ וְכַרְכֹּם קָנֶה וְקִנָּמוֹן/νάρδος καὶ κρόκος,
κάλαμος καὶ κιννάμωμον. The beloved's שְׁלָחַיִךְ /ἀποστολαί are
called מַעְיַן גַּנִּים בְּאֵר מַיִם חַיִּים/πηγὴ κῆπου, καὶ φρέαρ ὕδατος
ζῶντος (4:14).[25] Mary Magdalene's sending forth by Jesus is ironically connected to the reference of the lover in the Song to the
Shulamite's ἀποστολαι (shoots "sent forth" from a plant) as a
παράδεισος, an enclosed garden or paradise. Altogether there are
nine references to κῆπος and one to παράδεισος in the Song, and
two references to κῆπος and one to κηπουρός in the Fourth Gospel
(all in connection with Jesus' arrest and burial).[26] The garden setting
of the Song is an appropriate allusive backdrop for the encounter of
Mary Magdalene and Jesus.

Arise

After the disciples' visit in Jn 20:11, Mary stands once again at the
tomb. She looks inside and sees two angels. The description of their
seating arrangement confirms that this tomb resembles a small room.
In verses 12 and 13, the setting resembles that of the woman in SS
3:2-4. The searching woman says אָקוּמָה נָּא/ἀναστήσομαι as she
gets up to begin looking for her beloved in SS 3:2.[27] Although the
word is ordinary, it strikes an ironic chord in an exploration of con-

nections between the Song and the resurrection account. Mary Magdalene's response to the messengers who ask about her weeping is "they have taken away *my* Lord and *I* do not know where they have put him," personalizing her search significantly more than in 20:3.[28] Now she is the individual believer/lover seeking her Lord/beloved.

Voice

The Song and Jn 20 also share the theme of the power of the beloved's voice. In response to Jesus' voice saying her name, Mary Magdalene "turns" the second time and recognizes him. The Song often refers to the voice of the beloved, either directly or obliquely. The Shulamite says joyfully, קוֹל דּוֹדִי/φωνὴ ἀδελφιδοῦ μου (SS 2:8). Her beloved says, הַשְׁמִיעִינִי אֶת־קוֹלֵךְ כִּי־קוֹלֵךְ עָרֵב/ἀκούτισόν με τὴν φωνήν σου, ὅτι ἡ φωνή σου ἡδεῖα (2:14). The woman seeking her beloved gets up from her bed to look for him because, she says, ἐκάλεσα αὐτον καὶ οὐχ ὑπήκουσέ μου (3:1).[29] Again she speaks of קוֹל דּוֹדִי/φωνὴ ἀδελφιδοῦ μου in 5:2, and repeats in 5:6, קְרָאתִיו וְלֹא עָנָנִי/ἐκάλεσα αὐτον καὶ οὐχ ὑπήκουσέ μου.[30] The words of the woman in 5:6 also offer an intriguing reflection on Mary Magdalene's "turning" in Jn 20:16: opening the door to her beloved, the woman in the Song who has just heard his voice says, נַפְשִׁי יָצְאָה בְדַבְּרוֹ/ψυχή μου ἐξῆλθέ ἐν λόγῳ αὐτοῦ.[31] The allusive connection to this phrase clarifies Mary's reaction to Jesus' speaking her name; she is substantively changed by her recognition of him. Following the experience of the lover in the Song, Mary's soul went out of her at Jesus' word, if we understand στρέφω in its common metaphorical sense, to "change inwardly, to be converted, to change within and without." In addition, Bloch and Bloch suggest that the quality of SS 5:6 (נַפְשִׁי יָצְאָה בְדַבְּרוֹ) is best rendered, "I nearly died as he spoke." According to A. Bloch, "Here [נַפְשִׁי יָצְאָה בְדַבְּרוֹ] is a hyperbolical 'I nearly died,' expressing a deep emotional upsurge."[32]

Dweller in the Garden

In the Song of Songs' next to last verse (8:13) an unknown person addresses the one dwelling in the garden (הַיּוֹשֶׁבֶת בַּגַּנִּים/ὁ καθήμενος ἐν κήποις) drawing together the two themes of the garden and the voice of the beloved. It is not clear who is spoken to because the MT and LXX versions of the participle are of different genders. The Hebrew text of the Song would have been liturgically familiar to the community members most directly responsible for transmission of this story. In that case, the one dwelling in the garden is female, Mary Magdalene, and the verse then serves as a succinct recapitulation of the link between two beloved pairs, the Song's couple and Jesus and Mary. It also serves as a concise final connection between the Song and the Johannine narrative. SS 8:13b (חֲבֵרִים מַקְשִׁיבִים לְקוֹלֵךְ/ἑταῖροι προσέχοντες τῇ φωνῇ σου. ἀκούτισον με) effectively summarizes the apostolic proclamation, for Mary is sent to Jesus' companions to cause them to listen to her word about his appearing and his message to her. The verse serves admirably as midrash on the Johannine text. In the same midrashic vein, the final verses of the Song offer a theological summary of the resurrection appearance to Mary Magdalene and the content of her announcement to Jesus' sisters and brothers. The woman of the Song says כִּי־עַזָּה כַמָּוֶת אַהֲבָה קָשָׁה כִשְׁאוֹל קִנְאָה/ὅτι κραταιὰ ὡς θάνατος ἀγάπη, σκληρὸς ὡς ᾅδης ζῆλος (SS 8:6), which might describe the Johannine community's experience of Jesus' love for them that continued even after his death, and his passionate care for them even in the grave. Or, conversely, it could refer to the community's love for Jesus even in death and their continuing devotion to him even after his burial. The verse has many levels and layers at the end of a love story, and it connects two love stories.

Allusion opens a larger textual world, evoking a profound layer of meaning that not only clarifies the difficult aspects of the narrative, but also invites the reader to perceive the alluding text in a new way. Once the referent text is evoked, it becomes part of the story and must be seen in relation to the alluding narrative. Both the anointing and resurrection stories abound in allusions. In both stories there are notable instances of semantic indirection that bring the reader up short and, once their role as markers is perceived, lead the reader's attention to an evoked text. In both stories, the allusions point to the Song of Songs.

Notes

1   Jn 20:2-10 does not figure directly in this study and may stem from a different tradition from that represented by vv. 1 and 11-18. Believing that 20:10-20 was originally a separate story, R. E. Brown claims that three narratives may lie behind 20:1-18 (*Gospel According to John*, 998-999).

2   According to Schneiders, "the Mary Magdalene episode is the Canticle of Canticles of the IV Gospel" and that the Canticle is "the perfect model for John's presentation of the New Covenant" ("Johannine Resurrection Narrative," 362-363).

3   Schneiders asserts that the Song was used "thematically rather than textually," and that the Mary Magdalene scene is "NT Canticle of Canticles, not a citation of texts from the Canticle" ("Johannine Resurrection Narrative," 367, n. 86). However, my study shows that the Johannine resurrection narrative does have a substantial *textual* relationship with the Song.

4   M. Riffaterre, *Semiotics of Poetry*, 5-6.

5   Cf. D. Boyarin, "Inner Biblical Ambiguity," 44. Boyarin stresses that the choice of what one wants the text to mean is limited by what the intertext allows it to mean. J. Culler uses the term "naturalize a text" to mean "to bring it into relation with a type of discourse or model which is already, in some sense, natural and legible" (*Structuralist Poetics* [London: Routledge and Kegan Paul, 1975]: 138).

6   See Brown's summary of scholarship on Jn 20:14 and 16 in the *Gospel According to John*, 991. See also T. Baarda, "'She Recognized Him': Concerning the Origin of a Peculiar Textual Variation in John 20,16 Sys," in *Text and Testimony*, ed. T. Baarda, A. Hilhorst, G.P. Luttikhuizen, and A. S. van der Woude (Kampen: Uitgeversmaatschappij J. H. Kok, 1988): 24-38. Baarda discusses the Syriac variant in which Mary, instead of turning and speaking, "recognized him and answered and was saying to him. . . ."

7   D. Boyarin, *Intertextuality and the Reading of Midrash* (Bloomington: Indiana University Press, 1990): 41.

8   The MT's שׁוּב has the same double meaning as the LXX's στρέφω, implying either physical or spiritual and emotional turning. See W. L. Holladay, *The Root Subh in the Old Testament* (Leiden: E. J. Brill, 1958).

9   Boyarin claims that a series of verbal echoes suggests that a text is "intended as an imitation (or interpretation, from the hermeneutic perspective)" of another text (*Intertextuality and the Reading of Midrash*, 63).

10 The connection is no less strong if the Shulamite is urged to "dance, dance," as many commentators hold. The Mary Magdalene scene may have been a dance or liturgical drama among a sector of the Johannine community.

11   D. Boyarin, *Intertextuality and the Reading of Midrash*, 57.

12   Nestle-Aland 26th Edition *Novum Testamentum Graece* does not include the phrase in the body of the Johannine text, although its addition is supported by manuscript traditions that include ℵ Θ Ψ and more than one Vulgate and Syriac version.

13   See Brown, *Gospel According to John*, 992–993. The present imperative of ἅπτω indicates an ongoing action; "hold" renders this more accurately than "touch." See also M. R. D'Angelo's "A Critical Note: Jn 20:17 and Apocalypse of Moses 31," *Journal of Theological Studies* 41, 1990.

14   Schneiders takes a different approach to 20:17a, disagreeing with evidence based on the tense and mood of ἅπτω or the several possible negative effects of Mary's physically "touching" Jesus. She maintains that ἅπτω emphasizes the relationship rather than the touching itself ("The Johannine Resurrection Narrative," 441), and claims that Jesus is responding to the relationship implied by Mary's use of ῥαββουνι.

15   Robert Alter, *The World of Biblical Literature*, 113.

16   Ibid., 114.

17   A. T. Hanson is convinced of the relation between Jesus' command to Mary and SS 3:4, but he denies that this relation constitutes "an allusion that any well-instructed reader might be expected to recognize . . ." claiming that the reference to the Song is not an allusion because an allusion must be explicit (*The Prophetic Gospel*, 246).

18   Hanson's conviction about the relation between Jesus' command to Mary and SS 3:4 emphasizes what he sees as the Johannine need to show fulfillment of Scripture in everything in Jesus' life. Hanson claims that Jesus' charge to Mary Magdalene not to touch him can be traced to the Evangelist's belief that Scripture had foretold that she would touch him: "Perhaps at least part of the explanation for this mysterious command is that John found it foretold in scripture that she would seize Jesus, and he had to fit it into his theology of the risen Christ. No doubt an appearance of the risen Christ to Mary Magdalene was part of John's tradition. But it looks very much as if the actual details of the encounter have been strongly influenced, indeed one might say inspired, by the relations between the bride and her beloved in the Song of Solomon" (*The Prophetic Gospel*, 230). Hanson says, "the movements of Mary Magdalene at the empty tomb when she encounters the risen Lord in 20.14–18 seem to have been determined by the Song of Solomon 5.5–6 and 3.4 rather than by any historical tradition known to John" (ibid., 244).

19   The Synoptic resurrection accounts are found in Mk 16:1–8, Mt 28:1–10, and Lk 24:1–12. In the Marcan scene at Jesus' tomb (Mk 16:1–2), Mary Magdalene witnesses the empty tomb with two other women. However, the longer ending of Mark (16:9–11) specifies that Mary Magdalene was alone in receiving the first resurrection appearance of Jesus, although no details about this encounter are supplied. R. E. Brown notes that the Synoptic accounts, in

which a group of women come to the tomb, may be more plausible, "for a woman would not be likely to go alone in the dark to a place of execution outside the city walls" (*Gospel According to John*, 981).

20 Michel Cambe also notices the "striking" parallel between the scene in SS 3:1–4 and that of the appearance of Jesus to Mary Magdalene. Cambe notes that the scenes from the two texts have an identical design and that their backgrounds have similar elements ("L'influence du Cantique des Cantiques sur le Nouveau Testament," *Revue Thomiste* 62 [1962]: 17).

A. T. Hanson proposes that the description of the encounter between the risen Jesus and Mary Magdalene is based on two passages in the Song of Songs, 3:4 and 5:5–6 (*The Prophetic Gospel*, 229).

André Feuillet notes the relationship between Mary Magdalene's seeking Jesus and SS 3:1–4, and claims that this connection reinforces an ecclesiological emphasis. Citing the ancient allegorical interpretation of the Song as a description of the eschatological marriage of God and the chosen people, Feuillet claims it as confirmation that in this Johannine resurrection appearance Mary Magdalene represents the whole Church. Feuillet recognizes a number of the same textual elements mentioned by Cambe and Hanson, but he emphasizes their role as applications of Johannine ecclesiology ("La recherche du Christ dans la Nouvelle Alliance d'après la Christophanie de Jo. 20, 11–18," in *L'Homme devant Dieu* [Paris: Aubier, 1963]: 93–112).

21 MT חֶדֶר. The Hebrew text does not share the auditory dimension with the Johannine Greek that the LXX does, but the meaning of the Hebrew term for room in this verse confirms its similarity to the concept described by the Greek. חֶדֶר, is a dark inner room or sleeping chamber, a place of privacy and intimacy.

22 There is a similar play on words in one of Romanos the Melode's Hymns on the Resurrection:

ζωῆς ταμιεῖον,
χαρᾶς σημεῖον,
εἰρήνης δοχεῖον,
Χριστοῦ μνημεῖον

23 The MT has חֶדֶר in verse 3:4, but not in 8:2. Some commentators believe that this portion of 8:2 is corrupt and they emend it to follow the LXX's εἰς ταμίειον τῆς συλλαβούσης με (see A. Bloch and C. Bloch, *The Song of Songs*, 210).

24 The Fourth Gospel is also the only Gospel specifying that the location of Jesus' arrest was a garden (18:1), and Peter is asked if he was not with Jesus in the garden (18:26). The sole reference to κῆπος in the Synoptics is in Luke 13:19, the parable of the mustard seed.

25 There is similar vocabulary in Jn 4, especially the reference to "living water" in Jn 4:10, where Jesus offers the Samaritan woman ὕδωρ ζῶν, and she responds τὸ φρέαρ ἐστὶν βαθύ. πόθεν οὖν ἔχεις τὸ ὕδωρ τὸ ζῶν; (4:11).

26 SS 4:12 (twice), 4:13, 4:15, 4:16 (twice), 5:1, 6:2 (twice), and 8:13; Jn 18:1, 18:26, and 19:41 (twice).

27 See also SS 2:13, where the man says קוּמִי לָךְ רַעְיָתִי/ἀνάστα, ἐλθὲ ἡ πλησίον μου.

28 This change may also signal a change in the stratum of tradition, if there are three redactional parts to verses 1–18. C. Bernabé sees the plural form in 20:2 as an intentional reference to community ("Trasfonda Derásico," 215).

29 This phrase is not found in this verse in the MT.

30 Bloch and Bloch claim that SS 4:3 (וּמִדְבָּרֵיךְ נָאוֶה) also refers to "voice" (The Song of Songs, 170).

31 C. Bernabé believes that the "voice of the bridegroom" in Jn 3:29 reflects an affinity with SS 8:2 and 8:13. He maintains that the diverse allusions to the Song found in the Fourth Gospel are designed to culminate in Jesus' resurrection appearance to Mary Magdalene. He cites allusions in Jn 2:1–12 to SS 5:1, and in Jn 3:29 to SS 8:13, as well as the allusions in Jn 12:3 to SS 1:12, and Jn 20:1–18 to SS 3:1–4 ("Trasfonda Derásico," 209–210). See also R. Dillon, "Wisdom Tradition and Sacramental Retrospect in the Cana Account," Catholic Biblical Quarterly 24 (1962): 268–296.

32 A. Bloch and C. Bloch, The Songs of Songs, 182. Elsewhere בְּצֵאת נַפְשָׁהּ and תֵּצֵא רוּחוֹ are expressions for dying (Gen. 35:18, Ps. 146:4). The phrase here is compared to the woman's profound emotional "stirring up" in 5:4.

Chapter 4

The Song of Songs as Evoked Text

The previous two chapters illustrated the key literary links between the Song of Songs and the Fourth Gospel. These connections are evident in the vocabulary and images that the Song shares with the Gospel, and they become explicit when textual "bumps" invite the reader to recognize the coincidence of particular words and motifs. The prominence of the allusions to the Song in the Fourth Gospel makes it apparent that understanding the Johannine anointing and resurrection appearance narratives requires a grasp of the evoked text as well, for the Song is alluded to not just once or incidentally, but comprehensively.

Textual allusions are not merely decorations. They serve specific narrative, ideological, or theological purposes. The Evangelist's assiduous intentionality in alluding to the Song makes it necessary to investigate that book in its role as the evoked text. Investigation of the context of the evoked images within the Song reveals the effect of specific words, images, or motifs and shows that the Song's themes and vocabulary are analogous to elements of the Fourth Gospel. The Song's allusive literary relationship with the Gospel suggests that some other elements may also be related. Corroboration of the Johannine signals within the Song's own setting strengthens impressions about why the Song appealed to members of the Johannine community and what purpose it served for them. The shared narrative setting stimulates conjecture about the identity of the influential Johannine members who were responsible for alluding to the Song. Study of the Song itself confirms the likelihood that it is evoked in the Fourth Gospel. Although literary clues furnish abundant grounds for linking the Gospel to the Song, if the referents within the Song showed no resemblance in theme or setting to their presumed counterparts in the Gospel, considerable doubt would be cast on the connection. The Johannine intertextual relationship to the Song is *metonymic* and the allusions therefore intend to call up the entire Song. Investigation of key words in their context within the Song is intended to reveal both those aspects of the Song directly implicated by the Johannine allusions and the broader themes that inform the Song.

Hair

Hair is referred to directly in five places in the Song: 4:1; 5:2 and 11; 6:5; and 7:6 (and perhaps 1:10; 4:3; and 6:7—see below). The man's reference in verse 4:1 to the appearance of his beloved's hair as a flock of goats winding down mountain slopes is repeated in 6:5. Both these verses form part of the traditional *wasf* form seen elsewhere in the Song. With this poetic technique, the beloved's physical beauty is extolled by means of a systematic description of his or her body from head to toe or toe to head. The reference to hair in verses 5:2 and 11 concerns the man's wavy locks. In 5:2 the man begs to be let into the sleeping Shulamite's room, claiming that his locks (קְוֻצּוֹתַי/οἱ βόστρυχοί μου) are wet with the dew of night. In 5:11 the Shulamite refers to her beloved's locks at the beginning of her *wasf* about him.

In verse 7:6, the Song's final reference to hair describes the woman's flowing tresses holding a king captive. Pope, Murphy, and Bloch and Bloch attribute verse 7:6 to the man addressing his lover, while Falk ascribes it to the chorus of daughters of Jerusalem speaking to their friend.[1] In each case, the Shulamite's hair is described as a part of her overall physical appeal and the effect is to engage the reader further in the alluring delights of the beloved. This final reference to hair makes an explicit connection between the seductive physical attraction of the woman and her effect on the "king" who figures throughout the Song of Songs as one of the images of the beloved. Her hair holds him captive, either literally or, more realistically, in the metaphorical sense of "captivating."[2] There may also be additional references to hair in the Song. For example, M. Falk claims that בַּתּרִים (τρυγόνες) of SS 1:10 appropriately refers to the woman's *braids*,[3] although other commentators understand that the word connotes a kind of jewelry or circular ornamentation.[4] Bloch and Bloch also add a second reference to hair in 4:1, and they claim that 4:3 refers to hair, as does 6:7. In these three instances, where most commentators understand צַמָּתֵךְ (τῆς σιωπήσεώς σου) to mean "your veil," the Blochs advocate "your hair."[5]

King

The image of the king occurs in SS 1:1, 4, and 12; 3:7, 9, and 11; and 8:11 and 12, as well as in 7:6. It is unlikely that an actual king is referred to, in spite of the specific mention of Solomon in verses 1:1, 3:7, 9, and 11, and 8:11 and 12.[6] Although the Song is attributed to King Solomon in the superscription, few if any scholars believe that it dates from Solomon's time or that Solomon had any responsibility for it, nor do they take the references to Solomon in the poems as historical or consider the actual king a character in the Song.[7] Rather, the female protagonist's reference to her "king" here is another in the series of amorous titles. Commentators find the reason for the use of Solomon's name unclear and its function probably superfluous, a hyperbolic embellishment of the description of the beloved as king.[8] The verses are attributed to the chorus of daughters of Jerusalem or other unknown speakers.[9]

The first reference to "king" (1:4) occurs in the context of the woman's statement that the maidens love her beloved because his love is better than wine. She begs to be taken quickly by her king into his private room (חֶדֶר/ταμίειον).[10] In the second reference (1:12), the woman describes the king reclining at table (בִּמְסִבּוֹ/ἐν ἀνακλίσει). She is apparently nearby as he reclines, for she describes her nard giving its (or his) scent. In verses 3:9 and 11, the "king" reference is specific to Solomon and extols his extravagant luxuries and the joy of his wedding day when he was crowned by his mother.[11] It is unusual to see such a function given to a mother in the Bible, and in the Song the effect of this role is to emphasize the importance of the mother, already noted in other verses (1:6; 3:4 and 11; 6:9; 8:1, 2, and 5).[12] The Shulamite's frequent references to her mother include the wish that her beloved had the same mother so that they would be as close as brother and sister (and not troubled by outsiders, 8:1). In the context of the woman's desire to bring her beloved to her mother (3:4), the king's mother's involvement in a portentous role underscores the mother's significance in the Song as a whole, in contrast to the "father" in the Fourth Gospel.

The final specific reference to king comes in verse 7:6, noted above in regard to hair. Here the chorus (so Falk) or the man (so Murphy), delineate in the *wasf* form the beauty of the beloved woman, this time from her feet to her head. The portrait ends with the description of the woman's hair with the king caught in the tresses where "king" refers, as elsewhere, to the beloved man.[13] The implication of his capture may be taken figuratively, as the king's fascination with his lover's comeliness holds him enthralled, or it may be taken literally, as his physical proximity to his lover has caused him to become truly entangled in her hair. M. V. Fox finds corroborating details in ancient Egyptian texts where the boy character states that his lover's "hair is the bait in the trap to ensnare me"[14] and "with her hair she lassos me . . .".[15] In reference to the Song's female lover, Fox says, "She had made him a 'king,' and then captivated him by her tresses. . . . The youth in Canticles, being a 'king,' is trapped, most appropriately, by purple, the expensive royal cloth."[16] The Blochs also suggest the connection with images of entrapment in Egyptian love poetry and they confirm that the beloved "is her 'king' (1:4), and is 'held captive' by her long hair."[17] In 7:6, there is also a play on the MT's כַּרְמֶל, for the name of the mountain sounds similar to the name for purple cloth such as that worn by royalty. Further emphasis on the "purple" of the woman's locks underscores their appropriateness as a garment for a king.[18]

Myrrh, Nard, Scent

At least fifteen verses in the Song refer specifically to myrrh, nard, fragrance, or all three (1:3, 12 and 13; 2:13; 3:6; 4:6, 10, 11, 13, 14, 16; 5:5 and 13; 7:9 and 14). In 1:3 the woman's celebration of her lover's attributes includes reference to fragrant anointing oils and his name is compared to perfume. The smell of the beloved's myrrh is above all aromas, and his name is myrrh poured out. The references in verses 1:12 and 13 to the king reclining and then lying between his beloved's breasts are replete with suggestions of the aroma of nard. The woman declares that her beloved himself is like a pouch of myrrh (צְרוֹר הַמֹּר), or a bundle of myrrh (ἀπόδεσμος τῆς στακτῆς) as it lies between her breasts. Fragrance is mentioned in 2:13, this time the aroma of spring blossoms. Verse 3:6 describes the perfumed procession of merchants and of King Solomon, while 4:6 is the man's description of his lover's body as mountain and hill of myrrh and frankincense.

The sensation of rich aroma pervades the descriptions in 4:10, 11, 13, 14, and 16, where the man characterizes his beloved. Verse 4:10 mirrors the woman's discourse in 1:2-3, where she says "your love is better than wine; your anointing oils are fragrant . . ." Throughout the second half of chapter 4, the male protagonist describes the bride in terms of the scent of her clothes and the aroma of the fruits of her garden. In 4:13 the bride's shoots or buds are described as a garden or orchard (שְׁלָחַיִךְ פַּרְדֵּס/ἀποστολαί σου παράδεισος).[19]

SS 5:5 describes the woman rising from bed during the night to open the door for her beloved. Her hands drip with myrrh as she grasps the door handle. In the previous verse she had declared that when her beloved reached for the door latch, her innards stirred for him (וּמֵעַי הָמוּ עָלָיו/ἡ κοιλία μου ἐθροήθη ἐπ' αὐτόν), relating her feeling here to that expressed in 5:6 (see below, "I nearly died as he spoke"). In verse 5:13, the wasf she recites about her lover includes mention of his fragrant, spicy cheeks. The final references to aroma in the Song come in chapter 7, where the man calls the scent of his lover's breath like apples (7:9) and the woman refers to the fragrance of mandrakes over their love bower (7:14).

Feet

Two references to feet are found in the Song. The first, in verse 5:3, describes the woman's hesitation in getting up from her bed at night to open the door for her beloved. She says she has already disrobed, and washed her feet (רָחַצְתִּי אֶת־רַגְלַי / ενιψάμην τοὺς πόδας μου) and is reluctant to soil them again. This reference to feet is followed by the woman's decision to arise and open to her lover after he thrusts his hand into the opening and she longs for him. Her hands drip myrrh and she claims that her inmost being, or soul, has gone out at her beloved's word (5:6). Mary Magdalene's response to Jesus' speaking her name resembles that of the Song's Shulamite in SS 5:6. In Jn 20:16, Jesus calls the uncomprehending Mary by her name and she "turns" for the second time. While this "turning" is literally inexplicable, the voice of Jesus the beloved seems to generate in Mary a reaction analogous to that of the Song's lover, that is, "my being opened in response to his voice" (נַפְשִׁי יָצְאָה בְדַבְּרוֹ/ψυχή μου ἐξῆλθεν ἐν λόγῳ αὐτοῦ). As noted above, A. Bloch favors the reading, "I nearly died as he spoke." Coincidentally, the male lover in the Song, apparently having just spoken, "turns aside," and is gone (this is more easily seen in the MT וְדוֹדִי חָמַק עָבָר than in the LXX ἀδελφιδός μου παρῆλθεν).

The second reference to feet is found in verse 7:2, at the opening of a wasf describing the woman. Unknown voices, probably the daughters of Jerusalem, urge the woman to turn, or dance, or leap, and they admire her feet in sandals.[20] The woman's feet (or steps, פְּעָמַיִךְ/ διαβήματά σου) are beautiful as she dances.

Garden

While the specific references to a garden in the Song (4:12-13 and 15-16, 5:1, 6:2, 8:13) are relatively infrequent, the apparent setting of most of the poem is a garden, whether construed literally as the physical location of the lovers' interaction, or symbolically as the idyllic location of love's activity. The garden's heady fragrances crown the idyll. In the midst of such descriptions the man calls his beloved a locked garden, a sealed garden fountain, a well of living water (4:12-13, 15, 5:1). The enclosed garden symbolizes the woman's sexuality, which is not accessible to anyone but her lover. The Shulamite refers to her lover as a garden (4:16), and in 6:2 she tells the daughters of Jerusalem that her lover has gone down to his garden (probably referring to herself). The garden imagery is luxuriant and extravagant, giving the impression of rich sensual delight, realistically implausible for most gardens in the ancient Near East. The image suggests just the "paradise" (פַּרְדֵּס/παράδεισος) that the lovers provide for each other, the paradise of the first garden in Eden.[21] It also suggests the single-mindedness of love, as the garden is separated from all other earthly locations and the lovers are intent on each other.

The final reference to a garden in the Song comes in the next to last verse (8:13). The verse addresses the one dwelling in the gardens, but there is a disparity between the MT's feminine participle (הַיוֹשֶׁבֶת בַּגַּנִּים) and the LXX's masculine participle (ὁ καθήμενος ἐν κήποις), making it difficult to know who is speaking and who is spoken to.[22] The garden dweller is urged to let the speaker hear her/his voice, to which friends are listening. The dweller's ambiguous gender may have little effect on interpreting the Song itself since many of the verses are variously attributable to either the man or the woman indiscriminately. But the association between the Song and the Fourth Gospel leads to speculation on the connection of SS 8:13–14 with Jn 20:11–18. In SS 8:13–14, one dwelling in gardens, whether masculine (LXX) or feminine (MT), is addressed. The speaker declares that companions listen for this person and then urge him (and it is *him* in both texts) to flee, to go off. Both Jesus and Mary Magdalene are dwellers in the garden where the Evangelist specifies Jesus' tomb is found and their mutual companions (friends, disciples) will listen for their voices. The command to flee or go off (SS 8:14, בְּרַח דּוֹדִי/φύγε, ἀδελφιδέ μου) would be an appropriate response by Mary to Jesus when he declares that he must go to the father. It is equally conceivable as a part of Jesus' charge to Mary to go to tell the others about him, for he says to her πορεύου καὶ εἰπὲ (Jn 20:17).

Voice

Since the two lovers speak to each other throughout the Song and listen intently for each other's call, it is apparent that their voices figure prominently and fundamentally in the Song's theme.[23] Specific mention of the beloved's voice is found in 2:8 and 14, and in 5:2 and 6 (and perhaps 4:3). In 2:8 the woman expresses delight at the sound of her lover's voice (קוֹל דּוֹדִי/φωνὴ ἀδελφιδοῦ μου) as he comes bounding over the mountains. Arguments that suggest he could not plausibly be heard at that distance miss the point of the impression made on each lover by even the near possibility of hearing the other, even hearing within the soul. In 2:14 the man refers twice to his lover's voice, calling her a dove in the cleft of the rocks, expressing his longing to see her and to hear her voice, and calling her voice pleasant. In verse 5:2, which opens the section we have already seen in connection with "night" and "feet," the woman says that although she is asleep her heart remains awake. She hears the "voice" of her beloved as he knocks and he begs her to open to him.

Bloch and Bloch claim another reference to the beloved's voice in SS 4:3 (וּמִדְבָּרֵיךְ נָאוֶה/ἡ λαλιά σου ὡραία). While other commentators maintain that "lips" or "mouth" is the appropriate understanding,[24] the Blochs assert that the poetic parallel favors "voice."[25] This interpretation provides an additional connection between the Song and the Fourth Gospel, for the root of מִדְבָּר is the "word" of the Song's final mention of voice. It is an oblique reference in verse 5:6 in which the woman declares that her soul or inner being went out of her at the "word" (דָּבָר/λόγος) of her beloved.[26] While the exact term "voice" is not used in this verse, it is implied, and it connects with 4:3, where the "voice" is more than just speech. The expression may be understood in terms of the larger biblical meaning of דָּבָר and λόγος, suggesting the gift of the intrinsic being of the one speaking.

Turning

There are four references to "turning" in the Song, in verses 2:17; 6:1 and 5; and 7:1. The first comes when the Shulamite declares that she and her lover belong to each other (2:16), and she encourages him to turn to her (סֹב/ἀπόστρεψον). The ambiguity of the word itself (turning toward or away from the beloved) is resolved by the previous verse, but the significance of the phrase need not depend on discerning only one sense. Indeed, the double possibility allows one to understand the man either turning more entirely to his lover or turning toward the outer world knowing that he is safe in her love.[27]

Verse 6:1 is a question from the daughters of Jerusalem, who ask the woman where her beloved has gone, where he has turned (פָּנָה/ ἀπέβλεψεν). This time the turning refers specifically to the lover's physical turning (facing another direction) or his disappearance and the woman's search for him, a search that the chorus of women expresses willingness to join. The Shulamite tells the chorus (6:2) that her beloved has gone down to his garden, to the beds of aromatic plants. Like verse 2:16, above, which precedes an entreaty to turn, verse 6:3 affirms the lovers' possession of each other.[28] In verse 6:5, the man begs the woman to turn her eyes from him because they alarm or confuse him. For him, her beauty is so powerful that it overwhelms. The verse continues with his description of her hair flowing down her back.

The chorus of daughters of Jerusalem exhorts the woman lover to "turn" (7:1). The fourfold use of the word (שׁוּבִי שׁוּבִי הַשּׁוּלַמִּית שׁוּבִי שׁוּבִי/ ἐπίστρεφε ἐπίστρεφε, ἡ Σουλαμῖτις, ἐπίστρεφε ἐπίστρεφε) in a single verse suggests either an emphatic request to complete one action (for example, to turn toward the chorus) or else a directive—in this case more plausible—to perform the same action many times (for example, to turn round and round, or dance). Bloch and Bloch assert here that "the verb שׁוּבִי is not used in its primary meaning . . . but in the special sense of 'do again, do once more,' or 'go on doing!'"[29] The daughters' encouragement of the woman's dancing is the first line of the Song's only complete *wasf* about a woman. The delineation of the woman's attractive physical qualities begins with her sandalled feet (7:1) and moves up her body to her glorious crown of hair, sufficiently majestic to capture a king (7:6).

I Seized Him and I Will Not Let Him Go

Verse 3:4 is of special interest because of the light it may shed on the curious "do not touch me" of Jn 20:17. In the setting of the Song, this verse is not an unusual expression of feeling, but one the reader expects given the fervor of the woman's longing for her lover and the urgency of her search for him. The verse comes in the context of the Shulamite's description of the restlessness caused by her desire for her lover and it opens a brief narration of her search for him. It is not clear whether 3:1-4 describes a dream sequence or a waking exploration, but this is irrelevant to the significance of the verses. In a curious scene, the woman wanders throughout the city by night looking for her friend. One critic asserts that commentators' misgivings about the woman's recklessness cause them to reduce the narrative to a dream (or to suggest she must have waited until daylight). This observation could be applied as well to commentary about Mary Magdalene's decision to go to the graveyard at night, that is, that a woman should not do something so unsafe.[30] Repeating the refrain of seeking and not finding, she asks the city watchmen if they have seen the one she loves. Just then she finds him (3:4); she seizes him and refuses to let him go until she has brought him into her mother's house (אֲחַזְתִּיו וְלֹא אַרְפֶּנּוּ עַד־שֶׁהֲבֵיאתִיו אֶל־בֵּית אִמִּי וְאֶל חֶדֶר הוֹרָתִי/κράτησα αὐτὸν καὶ οὐκ ἀφήσω αὐτόν ἕως οὗ εἰσήγαγον αὐτὸν εἰς οἶκον μητρός μου καὶ εἰς ταμίειον τῆς συλλαβούσης με). In Jn 20:17, Jesus' command to Mary Magdalene that she not touch him is immediately followed by his statement that he has not yet gone up to the father (λέγει αὐτῇ ʼΙησοῦς· μή μου ἅπτου, οὔπω γὰρ ἀναβέβηκα πρὸς τὸν πατέρα). In a number of other places in the Fourth Gospel, Jesus speaks of the singular relationship he shares with his father.[31] The several explicit references of the Shulamite to her mother (1:6; 3:4 and 11; 6:9; 8:1, 2, and 5) and her mother's house are an intriguing counterpoint to the Johannine Jesus' father and his father's house.[32]

Night

The theme of night is associated with the two narratives of the woman's search for her beloved, both the account discussed just above (SS 3:1-4) and the account in 5:2-8. In these narratives the night theme is not conspicuously insisted upon, but it creates an atmosphere. Night is a time when one does not see as well as in daylight; its aura can be sinister or seductive, mysterious and private. For lovers, the night can provide peace and seclusion, or it can be a time of anxiety and apprehension, especially for one who does not know where her lover is. In 3:1, the Shulamite is in bed at night (בַּלֵּילוֹת/ἐν νυξὶν).[33] In 5:2, while the woman is in bed, her lover comes to the door and asks to be allowed in, emphasizing that his hair is wet with the dew of night (רְסִיסֵי לָיְלָה/ψεκάδων νυκτός). In both situations, the mention of night is presumably superfluous since it is the time one would expect the woman to be in bed. The explicit reference serves to underscore the mood.

Both stories show the woman going out into the city at night, thereby exposing herself to danger. The fact that she is willing to put herself at such risk confirms the urgency of her heart's yearning. So too, stress on the man's nocturnal arrival at her door makes it clear that there is an element of secrecy and intrigue.

Peripheral Themes

Other notable images in the Song suggest a peripheral relationship to the Fourth Gospel or invite speculation about values the Fourth Evangelist may share with the Song: the vineyard (SS 1:6 and 14; 2:15; 7:12; 8:11-12) and wine (SS 4:10), springtime (SS 2:10–13), and the man's frequent references to his lover as "my friend" (1:9 and 15; 2:2, 10, and 13; 4:1 and 7; 5:2; and 6:4).

There is no express mention of wine or the vineyard in the Johannine texts studied here. However, these themes are prominent elsewhere in the Fourth Gospel, in the story of the wedding feast at Cana (Jn 2:1-11) and in Jesus' farewell address to his disciples (Jn 15:1-6). In addition, the Evangelist implies that Jesus is to be identified as the bridegroom in his meeting with the woman at the well in 4:4-42.

While the season of spring is not specifically named in the Fourth Gospel, there is the explicit connection of the events in both Jn 12 and Jn 20 with Passover, a feast that occurs during the springtime. In the Song, this season is connected with the rebirth of the land and the renewal of life and love (SS 2:10-13); fragrant blossoms, young fruit, and wildflowers appear on the earth. The scene in the Song describes a time in which the earth arises from winter and the man who speaks, twice urges his friend to "arise" and come with him (2:10 and 13: קוּמִי לָךְ רַעְיָתִי/ἀνάστα ἐλθέ, ἡ πλησίον μου). Although the word "arise" is too common to claim that its use in the Song conclusively relates it to the Fourth Gospel, it does strike an ironic chord in a study of the Johannine resurrection narrative.

The feminine form of the Hebrew "friend," whose nine occurrences are listed above, is otherwise unattested in biblical Hebrew and conveys the impression of reciprocity and mutual companionship, just as the masculine form does.[34] Bloch and Bloch affirm that the lovers' use of the term רַעְיָתִי and its masculine counterpart "highlights the mutuality and reciprocity of their relationship."[35] Elaborating on the unusual male-female complementarity displayed in the Song, the Blochs note the reversal in verse 7:11 ("I am my beloved's and his desire is for me") of the traditional biblical attitude portrayed in Gen. 3:16 toward the relationship of the sexes. In Genesis, the trajectory of sexual desire is one-directional. The woman desires the man and the man rules over her. SS 7:11 inverts Gen 3:16 by making the woman the desired object: "and instead of the dominion of man over woman, the present verse speaks of a relationship of mutuality, expressed in a formula of reciprocal love like that in 2:16, 6:3." [36] This sense of equality is not only an integral component of the Song, but is also an essential part of the teaching and practice of the Johannine community.

Gender Roles in the Song

A textual study of the Song corroborates the abundant verbal links it shares with the Fourth Gospel. Investigation of the vocabulary and themes of the Song in their own right verifies the centrality of the Song verses evoked in the Fourth Gospel and the Fourth Evangelist's intentional connection of the anointing and resurrection appearance narratives with the Song. In no case has a key word or theme from the Song that is referred to in the Fourth Gospel turned out to be either irrelevant or irreconcilable with its Johannine context. But exploration of the context of the evoked verses naturally leads to further interest in dominant broader aspects of the Song. Study of the Song text, and especially the verses to which the Gospel alludes, inevitably leads to appraisal of the gender roles presented in the Song. The evidence of unusual, female-affirming roles also invites speculation about authorship. The Evangelist's allusions to the Song may be suspected of intending to include and affirm the attitudes that accompany the evoked texts. For this reason, it is important to explore more closely both how the Song presents gender roles and the poem's probable authorship.

In the history of modern biblical criticism, as early as 1857 C. D. Ginsburg made a forceful statement in which he claimed the biblical equality of women and men. Ginsburg used the introduction to his commentary on the Song of Songs to argue that the Genesis creation account "clearly states that the man and woman were created with the same intellectual and moral powers," and that "the woman was created with the same intellectual and moral capacities as the man."[37] Ginsburg extolled the Song as a celebration of the "virtuous example" of a woman. Just so, gender roles are more easily recognized in the Song from the attitudes implied in the text than from the activities of the characters.

The events which the Song describes take place in an idyllic setting which emphasizes the individual lovers to the exclusion of the social world surrounding them. The Song's woman and man are not portrayed carrying out the tasks that must have occupied the daily lives of Israelite young people. Such tasks are not the subject of love songs. The lovers' sole occupation and topic of conversation is enjoyment of each other. Consequently, it would be fruitless to seek evidence of distinctive gender roles based on traditional work expectations for each sex, or to say, for example, that the woman performs tasks more often expected of a man, or vice versa, because work is irrelevant to the lovers' interests. The only reference to an ordinary task for either lover is that of shepherd (SS 1:7–8; 6:2–3), and this is likely to be in symbolic service of the poem, although it may also refer to the couple's actual occupation. The reference to the man as "king" is entirely metaphorical. The couple's social setting is obliquely mentioned in SS 1:6, where the woman speaks of her brothers' anger about her impropriety, and 8:1–2, where she regrets her lover's unavailability to her in public (if he were her brother, however, he could be seen with her). In 3:4, the woman mentions her mother's house, where she apparently still lives, and in 5:7 she refers to being beaten by the city watchmen for being out at night. The equality of the relationship between the Song's lovers does not eliminate the cultural constraints on the woman's behavior.

The few indirect references to gender role within the concrete social milieu highlight a single striking attribute of the woman lover, her independence of both soul and body. The woman's own description of her behavior cannot be strictly realistic. Whether her reports of getting up from bed to seek her beloved describe dreams or waking experience (SS 3:1–4 and 5:2–7), the implication is that she is alone in her house or room and free to go out the door or bring her lover in the door. In reality, she probably shared her home with several family members whose sleeping bodies she would literally have to step over to reach the door, not the scene of intimate seclusion for which lovers hope. However, the contrast between a probable literal setting and

the woman's fantasy underscores her unusual autonomy of spirit under circumstances where such an attitude was unlikely to have been
encouraged in women. Her sense of independence and self-empower-
ment is conspicuous.

The reciprocity between the man and woman is one of the Song's
most unusual properties. Its prominence invites conjecture about the
attitudes of those responsible for writing, editing, and preserving the
Song. The female/male mutuality the Song presents is rare or nonex-
istent in other literature of the Hebrew Bible. Female voices are prominent in the Song: the woman speaks more than half its verses and the
female chorus speaks another tenth. The remaining third of the verses
are spoken by the male protagonist.[38] But it is not only female speech
that is conspicuous; not surprisingly, predominantly female concerns
are also apparent. Indeed, A. Brenner claims that there are portions
of the Song that are so redolent of the interests of women that they
could not have been imagined by a man. In her discussion of female
authorship in the Hebrew Bible, Brenner maintains that the Song provides significant indications of female authorship because "it contains
narrative sequences of real or archetypal experience, and its chief
figure (or figures) is that of a woman (or women)."[39] Whether or not
Brenner is correct in her claim that certain verses "reflect a woman's
emotions and world in such an authentic manner that no man is likely
to have written them,"[40] it is true that female characters who espouse
countercultural behavior may be suspected of being creations of female authors. There are verses that Brenner calls "so essentially feminine that a male could hardly imitate their tone and texture successfully," among which she includes SS 1:2-6; 3:1-4; 5:1-7; and 5:10-16.[41]
All of these verses figure in the Johannine allusions.

In the Song, female dominance of both speech and subject matter
causes the reader to experience the text as a singular affirmation of
women's experience and authority. The Song's literary and cultural
insularity allows it to portray gender roles without regard to social
exigency. C. Meyers has shown that the Song

> reveals a balance between male and female. The domestic setting allows for
> the mutual intimacy of male and female relationships to be expressed. . . .
> Neither male nor female is set in an advantageous position with respect to
> the other.[42]

Investigation of Johannine allusions to the Song in chapters two and
three reveals more than just a close textual connection. It also suggests a coincidence between the human relational expectations upheld

in the Song and those of the Johannine community. This coincidence
gives rise to speculation about attitudes the Johannine community
may have shared with the community that produced the Song. Jn
12:1-8 and 20:1,11-18 portray a confident assertiveness on the part
of women characters, as well as an attitude of mutuality on the part of
Jesus that was uncommon among men of his era. The evoked verses'
confirmation of the thematic correspondence between the Song and
the Fourth Gospel suggests a comparable understanding of gender
roles.

While the Song's unusual perspective on the behavior of the
Shulamite and her beloved is corroborated by aspects of Johannine
belief, there are allusions to the Song within the Hebrew Bible that
contradict the Song's message. For example, in an analysis of the
intertextual relationship between Hosea 2 and the Song of Songs, F.
van Dijk-Hemmes considers how the Hosean text uses motifs from
the Song to convey its own meaning.[43] She shows that the Hosean
text reverses the Song's viewpoint, and that almost universally male-
gendered readings of Hosea exclude recognition of the woman
character's point of view, with which a female reader might especially
sympathize.[44] Of course, the freedom of the interpretive process must
include the possibility of alluding to texts to use them against themselves, which the author of Hosea apparently did.

Van Dijk-Hemmes' intent is to reveal the inversion of the Song's
meaning in Hosea, in which the intertextual relationship becomes a
kind of parody. My study, on the contrary, shows the continuation of
an analogous meaning in the Song's use by the Johannine community. The two studies have dissimilar aims, but in both the search for
clues about gender roles is comparable, in providing evidence about
intertextual relationships and their intended effect on the reader. Both
the author of Hosea and the author of the Fourth Gospel showed
versatility and creativity in evoking the Song, and their ingenuity has
its effect on the reader.

The "quotations" of the Song in Hosea are a travesty of their original intention. Far from affirming the woman character's freedom and
independence, in their new context the allusions distort the Song's
message and, rather than uphold her experience, are held against the
woman. By parodying a text's original use, the author or editor of the
new text may intend to mock the previous context or to strengthen
the new context. The Song's use in the Johannine context is true to
its original intention. Evoked in the Fourth Gospel, the Song contin-

ues to affirm the experience of women as that of cherished human beings and of the reality of a compassionate, reciprocal response from a male lover.

The prophetic marriage metaphor in Hosea 2 presents a metaphorical relationship between God and Israel. The male character is presented as dominating and righteous and the female character as subservient and corrupt. In the Song, on the contrary, the lovers' relationship is one of both equality and virtue. M. V. Fox notes that

> equality is the essence of the relationship between the young lovers in the Song, and this can hardly have been intended as a model for God's relation to Israel (or to an individual soul). Patriarchal marriage, where the man initiates the relationship and provides for a woman, from whom he can then demand fidelity, is a more appropriate metaphor for the relationship between God and Israel and is so used by the prophets, most notably Hosea and Ezekiel.[45]

Fox addresses the characteristic understanding of the Song as an allegory for the relationship between God and Israel, explaining that the equality of the lovers in the Song, "where the only bond is mutual attraction and equivalent need," makes that relation an unsuitable analogy for the divine-human relationship. The dominance-subjection understanding of the divine-human relationship represents an attitude of patriarchy more than an accurate understanding of the relationship God desires with humanity, in either Jewish or Christian tradition. In his study of the relationship between the Song of Songs and Tamil love poems, A. Mariaselvam finds analogous cultural elements, including the equality of the sexes. He claims that

> the SS is a clear testimony to the equality of the sexes at least in the sphere of love-life. . . . One is struck even by the superiority of the female partner with regard to sobriety, initiative and responsible handling of the situations. The equality and mutuality of the woman with the man cannot be contested as far as the SS is concerned.[46]

Mariaselvam notes that the assertiveness of the female lover in the Song exceeds that of the Tamil woman, for in the Song (1:7-8) the woman initiates the rendezvous.

The portrayal of the equality of the gender relationships in the Song is one of its most apparent characteristics. This quality is significantly rare in the Bible and is sufficiently exceptional to invite speculation not only about gender roles in the text, but also about the text's authorship. The uncommon portrayal of the Shulamite's independence stimulates reflection on whose vested interests the text upholds and who was responsible for it.

Authorship

Information about the Song's authorship stimulates interest because of the light it may shed on the Fourth Gospel, given the literary link between these texts. The unusually autonomous behavior of the woman in the Song, combined with the abundance of verses she speaks and the distinctively female point of view she presents, arouse conjecture about the author. Similar considerations are notable in the Johannine anointing and resurrection appearance accounts. In those narratives, women have prominent roles and their behavior with Jesus is that of peers and intimate companions. They take initiative even under adverse circumstances. In Jn 12, Mary of Bethany's social impropriety provokes rebuke. Her spontaneous, abundant gesture of love confronts the usual cultural expectations. Although her behavior is socially outrageous, she is true to her own desire and anticipates the acceptance of her friend Jesus. In Jn 20, the grief-stricken Mary Magdalene behaves courageously. She goes out at night alone, converses with strangers in a cemetery, has a vigorous exchange with a man she thinks she does not know, and is guileless and genuine in her response to Jesus. Such qualities in the two Marys' behavior relate them to the Shulamite, just as the allusive textual links relate the Fourth Gospel to the Song.

Given the Song's ambiguous origin and uncertain dating, it is more appropriate to speak of who was responsible for the poems that make up the Song. M. H. Pope's otherwise exhaustive commentary on the Song does not directly address the question of possible female authorship. R. E. Murphy discusses the possibility of multiple authorship, but is inclined toward the likelihood that the literary unity apparent in the Song implies a single editor and possibly a single author of most of the poems as well. Murphy admits that little can be said about the authorship, date, or social provenance of the Song,[47] but he states that the Song's perspective is

> so strongly marked in comparison with views attested elsewhere in scripture that one is pressed to ask if the author may have been a woman; and surely she was, at least in part. It is the female protagonist, rather than the male, who speaks the majority of the lines, and she reveals her feelings more fully than does he.[48]

In reference to the beauty and literary cohesion of the Song, Murphy refers to the author or editor as "she."[49]

The question of authorship is, of course, more complicated than simply deciding whether this or that specific person wrote a piece. The issues involve probable influence on the content of the text, vested interest in retaining it, and the reasonable capability—through cultural forms or institutional practices—of preserving the work, rather than precisely who wielded the pen. Several scholars have addressed the complexities of discerning female influence on biblical texts and their conclusions are appropriate to this study of the Song as the subject of Johannine allusions. Texts in which female characters and speech predominate cannot for that reason alone be attributed to female authors. Women characters may also be presented by male writers, but they will then display traits and perform roles that reflect men's experience of women rather than women's experience. The Song presents substantive grounds for arguing that its author was female. More directly, there is the strong possibility that those who composed, preserved, and handed down the songs that became the Song were women.

S. D. Goitein's investigation shows that it is more prudent to speak of women's creation of biblical *genres* than women's authorship, since biblical texts may retain the imprint of their originators even when they are written down by male scribes. Goitein's examples include women as the bearers of news (the victory dance), women who mock the enemy, wise women, rebukers, prophetesses, dancers at the Lord's feast, creators of "whispered prayer" (Hannah in 1 Sam 1:13), dirge-singers, lamenters, and mourners. He describes several genres in which women's participation was paramount, among which he includes love poems and wedding songs, which he believes women created and performed.[50] Of course, male authors may have put these forms into women's repertoires, although their doing so may also reflect actuality. Goitein describes a "fragmented, jumpy and allusive form" as characteristic of folk poetry,[51] and he suggests that the mysterious "dance of the camps" in SS 7:1 (מְחֹלַת הַמַּחֲנָיִם/χοροὶ τῶν παρεμβολῶν) may refer to the "camp" of the young women on one side and the "camp" of the young men on the other, a ritual designed to facilitate matchmaking.[52] The implication is that the young women are the initiators; their activities are evident in those chapters of the Song of Songs in which

> the woman is the speaker, the thinker and the actor—and they are the finest and most original ones. The important thing is for us to see the Hebrew woman as *a creator of love poetry.*[53]

Goitein attributes much of the Song of Songs to the poetry of Hebrew women.

Van Dijk-Hemmes elaborates on the importance of avoiding confusion about the authorship of texts that describe women's activities or texts with prominent female characters. As she explains, such texts may not necessarily be written by women, for "the notion that texts *about* women were also written *by* women is valid only if additional and different arguments can be advanced." [54] The questions about gender roles and authorship are closely intertwined with regard to the Song. As we have seen, the unusual independence of the female character and the considerable number of female concerns lead the reader to suspect that women were responsible for the poems, whatever their role in the actual writing.[55] Bekkenkamp and van Dijk are more circumspect than Goitein about the freedom of women in ancient Israel, although they too see a strong female influence in certain biblical texts.[56] In seeking characteristics of this influence, they pursue a common basis for identifying clues to women's culture. They posit a critical question which is relevant to this investigation of the Song as the text evoked by the Johannine community: whether women's songs shed light on each other, "whether they develop and expand each other's themes."[57] They claim that

> the Song of Songs bears all the characteristics of women's poetry stemming from an oral tradition. It is lyrical in character, revolves around village and family, and is rich in imagery that cannot be described as mere details or *epitheta ornans*, but which determines the eloquence of the song.[58]

Bekkenkamp and van Dijk further specify that clues are found in the general, metaphorical or symbolic rather than literal expression of erotic experience; in the women's reference to each other as beautiful; in the repeated mention of the mother with no mention of the father; in the unimportance of inequality of strength; and in the initiating role of the woman.

Study of evoked words and phrases within their own Song context confirms their status as objects of Johannine allusion. The Johannine textual "bumps'" or markers' apparent literary connection with the Song is corroborated, and attitudes and themes evident in these Johannine narratives are reflected in the Song. These themes included unusually authoritative female behavior and self-assurance, as well as intimate reciprocity between male and female characters. Investigation of the context of the evoked text substantiates its relationship with Jn 12 and 20, and discussion about the unusual gender roles in the Song invites similar roles in the Johannine texts corroborates the evidence of literary links. Speculation about possible female authorship of the Song invites similar conjecture about the two Johannine narratives. It remains to discover the social context for Johannine evocation of the Song.

Notes

1   In M. Falk's assessment, 7:6 is the final verse in a poem that begins "dance for us, princess, dance . . .," which is more often rendered "turn, turn, Shulamite . . ." (SS 7:1). See Falk, *The Song of Songs*, poem 22.

2   As Falk renders it (ibid.). See, however, Mieke Bal's discussion of sinister imagery in biblical portrayals of the "lethal woman" (*Lethal Love: Feminist Literary Readings of Biblical Love Stories* [Bloomington: Indiana University Press, 1987]). Bal's treatment of the theme of hair and sexuality in the story of Samson and Delilah (Jud 16:4-22) is paradoxical, in contrast to my study of the Song. In the former story it is the man, whose hair represents sexual and physical power (power sufficient to "capture a king"), who loses his hair at the hands of the dangerous seductive woman. Several of the sexual symbols Bal addresses ("Delilah Decomposed" in ibid., 37–67) are identical to those found in the Song, but the Judges account presents them as contributions to Samson's downfall rather than enhancements to loving exchange between the couple.

   Absalom is another biblical character especially celebrated for his hair (2 Sam 14:25–26). As with Samson's hair, the influence of Absalom's beautiful hair on his fate paradoxically brings him to a tragic end (2 Sam 18:9–18). In the Song, however, the woman's "capture" of the king in her hair is presumably a desirable destiny for him.

3   M. Falk, *The Song of Songs*, 171.

4   M. H. Pope, *The Song of Songs* (New York: Doubleday, 1977: 343; R. E. Murphy, *The Song of Songs* (Minneapolis: Fortress Press, 1990): 134–135; A. Bloch and C. Bloch, *The Song of Songs*, 146. Murphy suggests that "one may derive some notion of this ornamentation from the . . . ivory plaque from Ugarit in which a woman seems to offer a jar of perfume to her consort."

5   A. Bloch and C. Bloch, *The Song of Songs*, 166–168. The Blochs compellingly argue that there is "considerable linguistic and textual evidence" for the interpretation "hair" rather than "veil."

6   Regarding the woman's reference to "king" in 1:4, A. Bloch says, "Here and in 1:12, 'the king' is to be understood as the Shulamite's courtly epithet for her lover. It is by no means a reference to King Solomon as a rival for her love . . ." (The Song of Songs, 138).

7   See Pope, 22–23, 432. Murphy and Childs, among others, believe that the attribution of the Song to Solomon serves the function of incorporating it into the sapiential tradition (Murphy, *The Song of Songs*, 121; B. Childs, *Introduction to the Old Testament as Scripture* [Philadelphia: Fortress Press, 1979]: 573–575).

8   M. Falk eliminates the name of Solomon from her translation. R. E. Murphy suggests that ". . . 3:6–11 seems to be somewhat of a foreign body within the

Song. . ." He claims that the "king fiction" is intended as a tribute to the beloved (*The Song of Songs*, 152).

9   See M. Falk, *The Song of Songs*, poem 14, and R. E. Murphy, *The Song of Songs*, 148.

10   According to A. Bloch, "The king's 'chambers' are best explained in terms of the lovers' vocabulary of make-believe. Since most of their erotic encounters take place out of doors, this word may designate the sheltered or hidden places in the woods or vineyards where they meet" (*The Songs of Songs*, 138–139). Bloch also notes that the expression חֶדֶר בְּחֶדֶר means "a chamber within a chamber, an inner chamber," or secret hiding place.

11   M. Falk comments on this verse's unique description of the role of the mother crowning her son (*The Song of Songs*, 180–181). Since this is not a function normally given to a mother, or to a woman at all, it may echo in the accounts of the anointing of Jesus' head by a woman in the Gospels of Mark and Matthew (Mk 14:3–9, Mt 26:6–13). There is the suggestion of a relationship between the mother of the "king" in the Fourth Gospel, Mary of Nazareth, and Solomon's mother Bathsheba, who is a prominent character in the Hebrew Bible. Both Mary and Bathsheba had influential roles in the inauguration of their kingly sons' missions (see, e.g., Jn 2:1–11 and 1 Kings 1:11–31) and although they are best known in their capacity as the mother of a famous king, they were also unusual women in their own rights (Mary less ambiguously than Bathsheba).

12   Bloch and Bloch refer to thematic connections in several places in the Song where the Shulamite's beloved is compared to the king, and there is a "prominent role given to mother figures" (*The Song of Songs*, 166).

13   In view of chapter two's focus on Jesus as the beloved held captive in Mary of Bethany's hair, it is notable that in *Song of Songs Rabbah* the king is equated with God who is held captive in Israel's tresses because "he bound himself by an oath that he would bring his Presence to dwell within Israel" (*Song of Songs Rabbah*, ed. and trans. Jacob Neusner [Atlanta: Scholars Press, 1989], 186).

14   *The Song of Songs and the Ancient Egyptian Love Songs* (Madison: University of Wisconsin Press, 1985): 9.

15   Ibid., 73.

16   Ibid., 161.

17   Bloch and Bloch, *The Song of Songs*, 204.

18   Bloch and Bloch discuss the use of "purple" to refer to the sheen of very dark hair (*The Song of Songs*, 203–204). They assert that "the enigmatic *rehatim* is generally viewed as a metaphor for hair.

19   The NRSV translates "your channel is an orchard of pomegranates," apparently understanding the difficult Hebrew (שְׁלָחַיִךְ) in reference to a water channel. Bloch and Bloch prefer "your branches are an orchard of pomegranate

trees," while M. Falk renders the phrase as a description of the bride stretching her limbs. In response to her gesture, a field of pomegranates blooms. According to Pope, "Christian interpreters, on the basis of the LXX ἀποστολαί [translated as channel] and Vulgate *emissiones*, related the apostolates and emissions of the Bride to the Church's arguments for the faith and its spread through preaching and planting local churches throughout the world, each of which is a paradise and replica of the original. The ἀποστολαί were also seen as the Apostles themselves . . ." (*Song of Songs*, 493).

20   The first-person plural verb in 7:1 (וְנֶחֱזֶה־בָּךְ/ὀψόμεθα ἐν σοί), although masculine in Hebrew, seems to be used in a general sense (see Murphy, *Song of Songs*, 181) and apparently refers to the chorus of women.

21   Bloch and Bloch understand פַּרְדֵּס as an "enclosed park": "the notion of an enclosure would fit well with the metaphor of the locked garden, 4:12" (*The Song of Songs*, 177).

22   Murphy does not consider the LXX variant "significant enough to modify the reading" in the MT (*The Song of Songs*, 194), and he chooses to allow it to remain ambiguous. Pope discusses the variant, but also chooses ambiguity of gender ("you who dwell," *Song of Songs*, 693). Falk (*The Song of Songs*, poem 31) and Bloch and Bloch (*The Song of Songs*, 117), who focus solely on the Hebrew text, retain "woman in the garden."

23   Bloch and Bloch note, "In the imagery of the Bible, a voice or sound—קוֹל can mean either—may be treated almost as an independent animate agent . . . Thus the eagerly waiting Shulamite may be referring to either the lover's voice or the sound of his footsteps" (*The Song of Songs*, 153).

24   See M. H. Pope, *The Song of Songs*, 463; M. Falk, *The Song of Songs*, poem 15.

25   A. Bloch and C. Bloch, *The Song of Songs*, 170.

26   M. V. Fox, however, repoints the MT to בְּדַבְּרוֹ, "because of him" my soul went out (The Song of Songs and the Ancient Egyptian Love Songs, 145–146).

27   According to M. V. Fox, "Opinions are divided on whether she is urging her lover to flee or to come to her to spend the rest of the night. . . . I am not sure whether she is calling him to her or sending him away, and I am not sure that we are supposed to be sure. But even a double entendre has a primary meaning, a meaning you are supposed to hear before you catch the hidden meaning. The primary meaning here is that he should flee. . . . there would be no point in the Shulamite's calling her lover to turn *to* her at a time when he was already facing her and speaking to her. So she is probably telling him to depart" (*The Song of Songs and the Ancient Egyptian Love Songs*, 115–116). Bloch and Bloch favor an interpretation in which "as daybreak approaches, the Shulamite urges her lover to hurry away, as in the aubade or alba of later tradition, where lovers part at dawn" (*The Song of Songs*, 158).

28   Verse 6:3 has the same construction as 2:16 and does not contain a word
     that specifically means "turn." Falk, however, renders 6:3 as she does 2:16,
     "I'll turn to meet my love,/He'll turn to me" (*Song of Songs*, poem 19).

29   Bloch and Bloch (*The Song of Songs*, 196). The Blochs accept the "wide-
     spread assumption" that 7:1 "begins a scene involving a dance by the
     Shulamite" (ibid., 195). Disputing the interpretations of other commentators,
     some of which require emendation of the text, the Blochs contend that the
     double imperative "can only be understood as 'Go on, dance some more!'"
     (ibid., 196). Pope renders the word "leap" and believes that שׁוּבִי is consistent
     with some aspect of dancing and need not connote "return" or "turn around"
     only (*The Song of Songs*, 595). Falk translates the word as "dance" and
     postulates a scene in which the chorus chants to accompany the Shulamite's
     dancing feet (*The Song of Songs*, poem 22).

30   Commentators are divided about whether the woman is describing a dream or
     a waking state. Murphy claims that "on my bed at night" merely specifies
     where the woman is, but without an explicit reference to a dream, there is no
     reason to think it is a dream. He concludes that "the situation is left vague,
     perhaps deliberately (as in 5:1), so that one cannot be sure if this is a dream,
     a poetic idealization, or reality" (*The Song of Songs*, 145). Pope says, "Many
     critics have felt that the scene cannot be real. The main objection is to the
     picture of the maiden scouring the streets at night in search of her lover" (*The
     Song of Songs*, 418). Pope explains that commentators' misgivings Falk af-
     firms that the SS 3:1–4 sequence describes a dream, and in her translation of
     these verses she consequently "tried to evoke a dreamlike atmosphere . . ."
     (*The Song of Songs*, 180).

31   See Jn 5:17–45; 6:32–65; 8:16–56; 10:15–38; 11:41; 12:26–50; 13:1 and
     3; 14:6–31; 15:1–26; 16:3–32; 17:1–25; 18:11; and 20:21.

32   Referring to the Song's mention of the "mother's house," C. Meyers notes
     that "the appearance of 'mother's house' is striking in view of the overriding
     importance of 'father's house' in the Bible. . . . In light of the importance of
     the concept of 'father's house' in Israelite society and the frequent use of that
     phrase in the Hebrew Bible, the appearance of 'mother's house' startles the
     reader" ("Gender Imagery in the Song of Songs," *Hebrew Annual Review* 10
     (1986): 218–219). See also Naomi's directive to her two widowed daughters-
     in-law to return to their mothers' houses (Ruth 1:8).

33   Both Murphy (*The Song of Songs*, 145) and Pope (*The Song of Songs*, 415)
     explain that the Hebrew plural has a singular meaning. Fox claims that the
     plural "in the nights" shows repeated action; in other words, he says, "the
     Shulammite has often lain in bed seeking her lover in her heart, yearning for
     him. This night she decides to get up and go out to look for him in the city
     streets" (*The Song of Songs and the Ancient Egyptian Love Songs*, 118).
     Bloch and Bloch also believe that in this context בַּלֵּילוֹת means "'night after
     night' in a frequentative sense" (*The Song of Songs*, 158).

34   See Murphy, *The Song of Songs*, 81.

35   Bloch and Bloch, *The Song of Songs*, 145.

36   Ibid., 207.

37   C. D. Ginsburg, "The Importance of the Book," chap. in *The Song of Songs and Qoheleth*, ed. S. H. Blank (New York: KTAV Publishing House, 1970 [1857]), 13.

38   There is some variation among scholars in the attribution of the verses.

39   "Women Poets and Authors," in *A Feminist Companion to the Song of Songs* (Sheffield: Sheffield Academic Press, 1993), 87.

40   Ibid., 89.

41   Ibid., 90–91. Although Brenner concludes that it is not possible "to determine with confidence which portions of the SoS express typical female attitudes with such fidelity that they can be regarded as original compositions by women," she asserts that "my personal guess is that passages such as 1.2–6, 3.1–4, 5.1–7 and 5.10–16 are so essentially feminine that a male could hardly imitate their tone and texture successfully."

42   C. Meyers, "Gender Imagery in the Song of Songs," 220.

43   F. van Dijk-Hemmes, "The Imagination of Power and the Power of Imagination," *Journal for the Study of the Old Testament* 44 (1989): 75–88.

44   Ibid., 75.

45   M. V. Fox, *The Song of Songs and the Ancient Egyptian Love Songs*, 237. N. K. Gottwald says, "Significantly, the man and woman are 'toe to toe' in their assertive acts and expressive words, a sexual quality which might equally bespeak the *comradeship of peasant lovers* not yet encumbered by children or the *companionship of upper-class lovers* whose affluence and education encourage feminist consciousness" ("The Song of Songs" in *The Hebrew Bible: A Socio-Literary Introduction* [Philadelphia: Fortress Press, 1985], 549).

46   A. Mariaselvam, *The Song of Songs and Ancient Tamil Love Poems* (Rome: Editrice Pontifico Istituto Biblico, 1988), 236–237.

47   R. E. Murphy, *The Song of Songs*, 5.

48   Ibid., 70.

49   Ibid., 91.

50   S. D. Goitein, "Women as Creators of Biblical Genres," *Prooftexts* 8 (1988): 1–33.

51   Ibid., 18.

52   Bloch and Bloch suggest a possible interpretation of SS 7:1 that involves two groups that face each other and are engaged in a dance, with the Shulamite dancing between them. While one group encourages her dancing, the other responds, "why do you gaze at the Shulamite?" (*The Song of Songs*, 195–196).

53   Goitein, "Women as Creators of Biblical Genres," 19.

54   "The fact that a woman appears as the main character in a literary work is by itself no decisive argument for female authorship. Heroines like Esther and Judith fit perfectly into a man-made gallery of ideal femininity. . . . There should, for example, be traces of a less androcentric intent; and/or of a (re)definition of 'reality' from a woman's point of view; and/or of a striking difference between the views of male and female characters-in-the-text." F. Van Dijk-Hemmes, "Traces of Women's Texts in the Hebrew Bible," in *On Gendering Texts: Female and Male Voices in the Hebrew Bible* (Leiden: E. J. Brill, 1993), 31.

55   As Brenner asserts, "Because of the predominance of the female voice(s) in the Song of Songs and because of additional factors, it is now commonly argued that female authorship—perhaps enveloped by male editorship—should be considered for the Song of Songs or most of it" ("'Come Back, Come Back the Shulammite'," in *On Humour and the Comic in the Hebrew Bible* [Sheffield: Almond Press, 1990], 273).

56   J. Bekkenkamp and F. van Dijk, "The Canon of the Old Testament and Women's Cultural Traditions," in *A Feminist Companion to the Song of Songs*, ed. A. Brenner (Sheffield: Sheffield Academic Press, 1993), 67–85.

57   Ibid., 73.

58   Ibid., 79.

Chapter 5

Social Context:
The Evoked Text as Antilanguage

This chapter's investigation demonstrates how the Johannine allusions to the Song of Songs exemplify a countercultural or "antisocietal" stance, such as that described by B. J. Malina. Malina's concept of the Johannine community as an "antisociety" provides a corroboratory vocabulary to explain the social function of the Fourth Gospel's allusions to the Song of Songs. Evocation of the Song functioned as a part of Johannine "antilanguage," the counter-cultural phenomenon in which people who believe they are outside the mainstream of society develop a manner of speech and a vocabulary that they alone understand and that excludes non-members.[1]

During the last twenty-five years, a fundamental change in the perception of the Fourth Gospel's historical setting has stimulated speculation about the social circumstances of the community responsible for that Gospel. Recent interest in this topic has centered on textual clues that give access to the Gospel's sociological context. As Malina has argued, the meanings encoded in the language of a text are derived from a social system, and the distinctive features of the Fourth Gospel reveal a social system presupposed by the Evangelist.[2] Reflection on the social function of the Fourth Gospel suggests that Bultmann's early speculations about the Gospel's relation to gnostic myth confirmed the Johannine community's desire for self-identity. R. E. Brown's research showed similarities between the characteristics of the Qumran and Johannine communities, and J. L. Martyn demonstrated the historical-critical basis for understanding the Fourth Gospel as a fusion of the horizons of the Johannine community with its own perception of the life of Jesus. W. A. Meeks described the context of the Johannine community as a symbolic universe whose central figure was the redeemer who came down from heaven and would ascend to heaven. The redeemer and his followers are distinct from the ordinary people of "this world" and the descent/ascent motif is dominant throughout the Gospel.[3]

The hermeneutical dynamic underlying the relationship between the Johannine community's self-definition and its method of scriptural interpretation are apparent in Malina's study of the social function of language and in Jerome Neyrey's investigation of theology as an expression of ideology in the Fourth Gospel. Malina postulates that the primary goal of human language is to form relationship, and he suggests two devices for situating the Fourth Gospel in its social location: identifying the type of story the Fourth Gospel tells and establishing the type of language the Evangelist uses in telling it. He adapts Mary Douglas' group/grid model in order to determine the social location of the Fourth Gospel, and he concludes that the Johannine community was highly individualistic and minimally adherent to external social structures.[4]

To assess the Evangelist's use of language, Malina uses Hayden White's model of historical explanation, or storytelling, where the storyteller arranges the story's elements in a sequence or temporal order, then "plots" the story, transforming it into a meaningful flow of action with a beginning, middle, and end, so as to give direction to the events. White suggests four basic modes of emplotment: comedy, tragedy, satire, and romance, and Malina decides that the Fourth Gospel is a romantic tragedy.[5]

By telling stories that advocate the same points in the broader social framework, historians affirm the social postures and way of life they (and the audience) wish to maintain. Stories are told in such a way that the reader or hearer takes action to uphold the social framework valued by the community: a story has an "ideological implication." The Fourth Evangelist's stories are intended to support the values of the community and to allude to texts that strengthen those values. The allusions to the Song of Songs uphold the ideology of the Fourth Gospel, underscoring that Gospel's support of intimacy, reciprocity, mutuality between the sexes, and lack of hierarchy. Seen as a "romantic tragedy," Malina says, the Fourth Gospel demonstrates a mode in which social interruption is necessary because the community's values do not match its experiences. The Gospel's formal argument highlights the uniqueness of individuals and individual actions in the story; there are few general descriptions.

Neyrey uses Malina's adaptation of the Douglas group/grid model to explore the Fourth Gospel's social location. Focusing on the Gospel's high Christology, he wants to discover "how spirit can function as a code word or symbol for a strategy of revolt."[6] He hypothesizes that the Johannine community's progression from low to high christological confession mirrors its change in attitude toward the surrounding culture. His research illuminates the process by which Johannine Christians formed a theology in response to their perception of their own identity. Johannine allusions to the Song reflect this theological choice.

The conclusions reached in recent Johannine scholarship overwhelmingly favor a view of the Fourth Gospel community as internally focused and highly sectarian with regard to both the outside world and other Christian communities. Johannine Christians thought of themselves as special, as the privileged recipients of the redeemer's message. They had an extreme sense of separation, election, and identification of their own community's experience with that of the earthly Jesus, to the extent that their story fused the two experiences. On the whole, recent studies agree that Johannine Christians were exclusive and isolated, unique, individualistic, and minimally adherent to social structures.

The experiences described in Jn 12:1–8 and Jn 20:1,11–18 are distinctive with regard to the other Gospels and they exemplify an individualism and autonomy on the part of women that is compellingly countercultural. Malina's treatment of Johannine antilanguage confirms the present study's findings, but Jn 12 and 20 contrast with much of the Fourth Gospel in focusing on notably physical endeavors. Jn 12 does not portray Jesus as an otherworldly redeemer, but depicts him as an ordinary human being at a social gathering with friends. While the Jesus whom Mary Magdalene encounters in Jn 20 is understood by the reader to be resurrected from death, and therefore no longer of the earth, this same Jesus' encounter with Mary is quite earthly. While some portions of the episodes are indeed enigmatic, their puzzling nature derives more from confusing gestures and conversation than from an esoteric theology.

The earthiness of the episodes studied here follows from an inversion of the phenomenon described by Neyrey. His conclusions about the correlation among community alienation, "otherworldliness," and high Christology prompt speculation about the Fourth Gospel's descriptions of physical human experience such as those found in Jn 12 and 20. The strata Neyrey describes show the increasingly high

Christology of the Fourth Gospel's later stages and mirror the community's growing sense of separation, while the texts studied here represent an early period in Johannine history. The highly individualistic nature of the community is already evident, as is its emphasis on interpersonal relationship as the primary manifestation and expression of faith. But the ethereal and intellectual abstractions with which the Fourth Gospel is strongly identified are notably lacking in the anointing and Magdalene appearance accounts. In these narratives there is, instead, an abundance of concrete human detail involving the physical senses (especially smell and touch), and Jesus is portrayed in a solidly human aspect.

The account of the raising of Lazarus (Jn 11:1–44) involves the same household as the anointing story (to which it refers in 11:2). The emotional engagement of Jesus and the other characters in the Lazarus story contributes to that account's exceptional earthiness, even with its description of a miracle of unimaginable magnitude. The narrative features precise descriptions of the experiences of the senses as well (e.g., weeping, 1:33; bursting into tears, 1:35; profound inner disturbance, 11:38; stench, 11:39). With the removal of the enigmatic words of Jesus in 11:9–10 and the high christological speech in 11:24–27, the story is a simple and concrete account of human grief and compassion. The human friendship that initially drew particular Christians together had not yet developed into a fiercely separatist stance in regard to other believers. The prominence of women in Jn 12 and 20 (and 11), where they are clearly leading characters, may imply the tales' oral origin within these women's communities. This tendency has been observed in the Song of Songs, where women are traditional collectors and conservators of certain stories and songs. In a community that produces a text like the Fourth Gospel, there must be many members whose experience of God in Jesus is expressed less abstractly than that described in much of the Fourth Gospel. These members will honor their own experience.

Allusions to the Song as Speech Accommodation

The sectarian nature of the Johannine community and its high Christology, preference for the "spiritual," and increased separatism appear in inverted form in the low Christology and earthiness of the Jn 12 anointing and Jn 20 appearance accounts. The lavish corporeality of the Song of Songs is allusively evoked in Jn 12 and 20 and enhances the physical and sensual essence of those stories, including their indications of the humanity of Jesus. References to the Song not only amplify the images of the Johannine narratives, but they also have a role in the cryptic speech of Johannine Christians, their antilanguage. While Neyrey's study shows how the spiritual sphere functions increasingly as a code for revolt in the Johannine community, the Gospel's immersion in the bodily realm and the humanity of Jesus also served as an ideology for certain Johannine members. Malina's study of antilanguage in the Johannine community confirms the social context for the Fourth Gospel's allusions to the Song.

Linguistic Convergence and Group Identity

Malina enlists speech accommodation theory to explain some of the idiosyncrasies of the Fourth Gospel. Citing the author's need, especially in the ancient world, to be heard favorably by the audience, Malina explains how the Fourth Gospel can be understood as a bid for social approval as well as an expression of profound faith. Referring to the "three-tiered" model of language,[7] Malina says that the Bible reader must ask about the social system or social meaning expressed in the text.[8] He demonstrates speech accommodation theory's basis in the recognition of the human desire to adapt one's language to the language of those with whom one is speaking. Authors who have a positive view of their audiences want to draw nearer to them; they are therefore attentive to the language the audience needs to hear.[9] This adaptation of language (or social convergence[10]) has implications for discovering who the listeners (or readers) are. Listeners who are motivated to continue listening already have a sense of what their conversation partners are going to say because their social context limits the possibilities. If "communication is a process of linguistic convergence,"[11] then allusion to the Song must be understood as part of the Evangelist's bid for communication with the audience. Hearers or readers of the Fourth Gospel expected allusions to the Song because reference to a text like the Song could be anticipated given the listeners' frame of reference. Devout hearers of Scripture would always expect scriptural texts to refer to other Scripture, either directly or by oblique evocation. It is not the fact of the allusion so much as the choice of evoked text that reveals the audience to us.

The Johannine Community as an Antisociety

The story of the life, death, and resurrection of Jesus, presented in different versions by the communities of the early Church, was in every case a challenge to the thought of the ancient world. The version of the story presented in the Fourth Gospel was, if anything, more difficult to accept than the distinctly different Synoptic accounts. Part of the difficulty it presented was its manifest in-house focus, its exclusive appeal to members of its own group, its evident unconcern for either non-Christians or other kinds of Christians. Apparently copying or sharing a cryptic and esoteric vocabulary associated with other ancient worldviews, the Evangelist was un-communicating as much as communicating. That is, very few can have understood what was being said. Even so, the story told must be assumed to have appealed to an audience who did understand it. The Evangelist wanted to recount an important but implausible narrative and wanted, as well, to gain social approval. We must presume, according to what we know of the social context of the ancient world, the anticipation of an audience of kindred spirit. As Malina contends, "In Jn's case, the author adequately revealed who he thought his audience was and what sort of language they would understand."[12] It is sensible to suppose that the Gospel's original audience understood the author's assessment of the characters and interactions depicted.

The Evangelist converged linguistically toward the audience—and diverged linguistically from the non-audience, that is, from those who were not in the community. Those who understood the Fourth Gospel were resocialized and became able to understand "Johannine." People who do not wish to be understood by outsiders deliberately dis-accommodate them. The Johannine community did not welcome or want to resemble the mainstream. They also diverged from other groups and used language in order to maintain their distinctiveness. The community's distinctive language and self-identification and its weak group/low grid status (highly individualistic and minimally adherent to external social structures) are symptomatic of an antisociety.

An antisociety, as the name suggests, is a group that adheres to a social structure whose values contrast with those of members of the prevailing society. Members of the antisociety exist within the larger culture from which they are alienated. According to Halliday, an antisociety is a society that is set up within another society as a conscious alternative to it. It is a mode of resistance, resistance which may take the form either of passive symbiosis or of active hostility and even destruction.[13]

Antisocieties show consistency in their characteristics regardless of the diversity of their cultural and temporal milieus. Members of antisocieties—who may be criminals, prisoners, students, vagabonds, and so on—develop ways of speaking among themselves and they resocialize, or create an alternate reality. Their antilanguage is a significant means by which they implement resocialization, for it "serves to create and maintain social structure through conversation, just as an everyday language does," but it has "a special character in which metaphorical modes of expression are the norm . . ."[14] An effect of the use of antilanguage is, of course, that outsiders will not understand it. The lack of understanding is not the primary purpose of the antilanguage, but it is inevitable given that the alternative reality it describes is a "*counter*-reality set up in *opposition to* some established norm."[15]

Antilanguage in the Fourth Gospel

Malina's argument that the Johannine community fits the criteria of an antisociety depends on the social system concealed within the language of the Fourth Gospel. The Gospel teaches us more about its readers than about its author or the document itself. Just as this study of the Johannine poetics of allusion starts at the basic level of words, Malina also begins with words to determine what concerns could explain the text of the Gospel. He finds the Gospel's focus summed up in Jn 20:31,[16] and he asserts that the Evangelist aims to develop in Fourth Gospel readers an "emotional anchorage 'in Jesus'" by "relexicalizing" ordinary vocabulary, using distinctive, deceptively simple words, and an abundance of apparent synonyms for the terms. Social values are highlighted and underscored in an antilanguage. The Johannine anointing and resurrection appearance accounts exemplify these antisocietal modes of meaning and the evoked Song of Songs serves just the purpose required in the antilanguage scheme.

One of the key requisites of antilanguage is its focus on the interpersonal. Martyn's research on the historical location of the Johannine community led him to see the Fourth Gospel as a layered document whose "story" was as much that of the later community as it was of the earthly life of Jesus of Nazareth. Curiously, however, the hostility that Martyn noted in opponents of the Johannine community does not seem to be predicated on specific beliefs held by that community. Rather, it is the community's antisocietal stance and "special" relationship with Jesus and God that are the source of the animosity. There is no substantive *content* to the opposition, just as there is no apparent content to the criterion for membership. Johannine membership is entirely a question of relationship, and it makes sense for this community to allude to the Song of Songs whose love-song genre obviates the need for rational content. The Song is an extended expression of interpersonal relationship and an excellent example of overlexicalization.

Malina says that "Jn's Gospel reflects the alternate reality Jn's group set up in opposition to its opponents . . ."[17] The role of antilanguage for the Fourth Gospel group, as for any antisociety, is to reinforce their alternate reality, as well as to exclude those who are not "their own." A key to understanding the message of the Fourth Gospel is found in its focus on communication and relationship, with little overt attention to substance. Johannine Christian attitudes and relational expectations—such as "love"—are easy to delineate, but there are few specific tenets of Christian faith. Since an antisociety exists within the larger culture and since its continued existence depends on its countercultural stance, antilanguage reinforces the continued articulation of "love" among the group members in the midst of oppressive circumstances, and it strengthens the essential affective connections. The connections do not take place by means of appeals to the intellect, but by ordinary conversation, "the most important vehicle of reality maintenance."[18]

The resocialization process is profoundly dependent on conversation, whose presentation of reality is implied more than stated. The literary use of allusion is based on implication, on not quite spelling out one text's relation to another, thereby creating an ambiguity that appeals to the imagination. The antisocietal reader or hearer will catch the ambivalent possibility and know from the connection to the group what is meant. Jn 12:1–8 and 20:1,11–18 are conversational interactions between Jesus and a disciple (Jn 12:1–8 is a non-verbal conversation), serving to resocialize. Not only is such Johannine speech based chiefly on affect, it is often incomprehensible in terms of any ordinary linguistic interchange, even that of other Christian communities (Synoptic or Pauline, for example). Such Johannine speech, Malina says, is not "meaning-bearing language" in the normal sense, but is intended to generate or describe relationship.

The Johannine anointing at Bethany shares some salient aspects with the Synoptic accounts, but crucial elements of the story are unique, such as the name of Mary of Bethany as the anointer (and her previously identified relationship with Jesus in Jn 11:2), the anointing of Jesus' feet rather than his head, the absence of tears, Mary's wiping of Jesus' feet with her hair, and the ointment's smell filling the house. In the Johannine account of Jesus' resurrection, Mary Magdalene comes to the tomb alone (in contrast to the Synoptic group arrival). Her subsequent conversation with the risen Jesus, her abundantly clear emotional engagement with him, her implicit attempt to touch him, and Jesus' personal commission to her, are affective narrative aspects not found in the Synoptic accounts. These particulars illustrate Johannine antisocietal linguistic details like those exemplifying antilanguage. Just as the allusions to the Song in these conversations are not explicit, so is the reality they maintain grasped only by the initiates.

It is essential to note the *metaphorical* nature of antilanguage. While regular language uses metaphor as a part of its means of expression, antilanguage *is* metaphor.[19] Because metaphor is ambiguous by nature, it is an effective means of disguising the communication of members of an antisociety and of supporting their in-group connection. The *casual* nature of conversation belies its powerful impact since its form may be casual even when its subject matter is profound. The encounters described in Jn 12 and 20 are casual in that they are spontaneous and unplanned, but their significance is no less consequential for their informality.

Antilanguage and Intimacy in Jn 12 and 20

Specific details in Jn 12 and 20 and their allusions to the Song demonstrate both how the sociolinguistic process functions and what it reveals about the Johannine milieu. Demonstration of Fourth Gospel allusions to the Song within a plausible social context not only broadens understanding of these allusions' function for the Johannine community, but also reveals their powerful role in the maintenance and reinforcement of the Johannine construction of reality. Intimate communication is a foundational concern in the uniquely Johannine rendition of Christian belief, whose only tenet is that disciples must love

Jesus and one another. This bond of love is the ultimate in social convergence. The Song of Songs' inclusion in descriptions of intimate encounters confirms the author's understanding that it expresses a desirable attitude toward human relationship. By the same token, a dominant function of Johannine antilanguage must be to foster intimacy.

The Fourth Evangelist's language moves consistently toward greater intimacy. My findings about Jn 12 and 20 demonstrate how these texts exemplify the "dimensions of communication associated with relationship development." [20] The allusions to the Song amplify the dimensions of communication and are integral to the Evangelist's narrative. The in-group receives increasing messages. Members of the Johannine inner circle are the recipients of privileged information that is not available to outsiders. In the Fourth Gospel, in contrast to the Synoptics, the anointing account is set in the home of members of the inner group of those who are close to Jesus. The Bethany family who are privileged to receive Jesus as a guest in their home are members of the circle of Jesus' special friends (12:1–2).

At the end of the account of Jesus' appearance to Mary Magdalene, Mary is sent by Jesus to "my brothers and sisters" (20:17b), not to the whole world. She is directed to give them a special (Johannine) message from Jesus that presumably only insiders can understand. She goes "to the disciples" (20:18) and pronounces the Johannine credential formula, "I have seen the Lord" (20:18b). The "these things" Mary claims Jesus told her are like the "many other things" of 21:25, which Malina concludes are related to the "things" known by the Johannine community but not by outsiders.

In interpersonal contact, persons who do not know each other well use highly stylized behavior, whereas familiars share the personal and individual communication of intimates. The exchange between Mary of Bethany and Jesus in Jn 12:3 reveals a presumption of striking intimacy and exceptional relationship. The fact that nothing is said between the two only heightens the uniqueness of their interchange. Mary's anointing Jesus' feet with expensive ointment and, especially, her wiping his feet with her hair are "personalized communication devices" of an extraordinary sort. They indicate an exceptionally familiar relationship between the parties. The allusions to the Song intensify this sense by bringing the reader more deeply into the world of fragrance, flowing hair, and the lavish title of King for the beloved. Without the allusion the intimate kingly title would be lost to the reader since it does not appear in the Johannine text itself. In contrast to Mary's action, Judas' stylized speech about "the poor" (12:4–5) and his lack of friendly gesture toward Jesus (or toward anyone else in the narrative), as well as his attempt to discredit the affectionate exchange, make it clear that he moves in the direction of less intimacy.

Jn 20:1,11–18 also describes a peculiar interaction that illustrates intimate communication. Because it begins with non-communication between the partners, the sudden turn to intimate interchange is startling and effective. The reader expects intimacy after a Gospel-long history of such relationships between Jesus and his disciples. This expectation heightens the stylized atmosphere of the opening exchanges in this resurrection narrative. Mary Magdalene encounters two unknown persons who greet her formally (20:12–13), addressing her as γύναι. She replies formally in spite of her distress, referring to κύριον μου rather than calling Jesus by name. Her sorrow has resulted in a feeling of acute estrangement that contradicts the familiarity the reader has come to presume. So too, the Song's seeker, whose search is evoked here, is thrust out of her normal world of intimate communion, confounded by suffering (SS 3:1–4).

Jesus' words to Mary Magdalene, like the angels', begin in a stylized manner; he also addresses Mary as γύναι. She responds formally again, calling Jesus κύριε. The unique communication patterns that Johannine disciples share with their Lord have still not broken through Mary's grief-induced disorientation. It is Jesus who effects the break: he calls Mary by her name, suddenly and without preamble (20:16). His abrupt move in the direction of uniqueness disintegrates the stylized mode and shifts the dialogue to intimacy. Mary responds with a term of familiar affection, ῥαββουνι. Allusions to the Song underscore the re-establishment of intimacy by recalling the power of the beloved's voice in the garden (which figures as the setting of uniqueness in the Song).

Communication is more efficient and accurate as the intimate context increases. The encounter between Jesus and Mary of Bethany (Jn 12:3) can only occur because of the exceptionally high context they share. The first-century cultural expectation for women's modesty precluded such an egregious breach of convention as Mary's wiping Jesus' feet with her hair. Jesus' apparent approval of her deed merely added insult to cultural injury. But both partners operated in a setting of heightened expectation of intimacy; neither spoke because the high context did not require that anything be "spelled out." In contrast,

Judas, as an outgroup person, did not share in the intimacy. He therefore felt obligated to explain and clarify (Jn 12:6) and Jesus had to "spell it out" for him (Jn 12:7–8). Judas' outburst may have been due to a previous high context relationship with Jesus which, as Malina suggests, may become overconfidence and may turn to misunderstanding in a new period.

In the appearance account, what begins as a low context setting because of Mary Magdalene's misunderstanding quickly changes to high context once Mary becomes aware of the new situation. The context's change in exterior manifestation first confuses Mary, perhaps as a result of the same phenomenon of overconfidence that troubles Judas in Jn 12:5. Mary's confusion results in "turning, turning" until Jesus speaks a word of re-contextualization, her name. The result is Mary's return to a high context in which she feels free to touch Jesus without warning (Jn 20:17). Both pericopes' allusions to the Song amplify the high context setting because the relationship of lovers is that of the highest possible context, where virtually nothing has to be explained in the most intimate moments, moments that fill the Song. The Song's sensual images and motifs underscore a context where the very flora and fauna provide an environment of intimacy that speaks on behalf of the lovers.

People who know each other well communicate the same idea in several different ways. Those who do not know each other or who are ending a relationship are more rigid in their choice of expression. Flexibility moves toward intimacy; rigidity maintains or causes distance. Mary of Bethany easily moves to a new demonstration of affection with Jesus, and Jesus easily receives it. Although it is unlikely that such an expression had been offered before, both partners are prepared for it because their close relationship allows for exceptional flexibility. Judas, on the other hand, is ending his relationship with Jesus and is in the outgroup. He consequently has a rigid worldview that allows for only certain appropriate behavior. Mary Magdalene begins in the rigid stance because she thinks she is dealing with someone she does not know (the gardener), but she quickly reverts to her former ingroup flexibility when she recognizes Jesus and seizes him. Perhaps his admonition in Jn 20:17 must be understood as a kind of flexibility of loving expression, contrary to what a beloved would expect but finally acceptable because lovers' behavior to each other is always in the high context of love. Once again, evocation of the Song augments the sense of flexibility between familiars in contrast to the more rigid behavior of outsiders (e. g., the watchmen in SS 5:7 or the woman's brothers in 8:8–9).

Intimates are inclined to fuse with each other, whereas new acquaintances are awkward. Jesus understood what Mary of Bethany was about; perhaps he knew immediately when she came toward him with the pot of ointment even though the event had not happened before. The Jesus character in the narrative—as a member of the Johannine social context—would have intuitively recognized the start of a gesture designed to increase attraction. Mary of Bethany's wiping Jesus' feet with her hair must indubitably be classified as a "smooth," self-confident gesture in anyone's lexicon. Mary Magdalene may have understood herself to be invited to touch Jesus because of the instinctive "inclination toward fusion" of intimates. The Evangelist's allusion to the Song at this crucial point in the narrative serves to emphasize both the naturalness of Mary's expectation and the shock of Jesus' rebuff since he surely anticipated her embrace in such a privileged high context (see above). Johannine readers recognized the allusion to SS 3:4 and anticipated that the woman would "hold him and not let him go." Without the evocation of the Song's seeking lover, there would be no reason to foresee an embrace and consequently no impact in Jesus' refusal to be touched.

The public presence, or persona, is the aspect that is revealed to everyone. It is how one wishes to be perceived by those who do not know one well, by the world. The move toward intimacy is seen in the gradual revelation of personal aspects of oneself. It involves an increase in physical closeness, in touching (especially private areas), and a relaxed demeanor. This portrayal of personal revelation applies without reservation to love poetry like the Song. What is unusual is how clearly it applies to the Johannine texts that allude to the Song. It is evident from Jn 12:1–8 that Mary of Bethany dramatically increases her proximity to Jesus by sitting or kneeling at his feet, and apparently remains there for several minutes. Mary touches Jesus' bare feet with her hands as she anoints them and probably looks at them intently while she anoints. She exposes her hair to Jesus and touches this normally "inaccessible body part" to his feet (the hair of a first-century Palestinian woman was a "private part"). It is reasonable to suppose that Jesus may be gazing at her while she anoints him. No bodily tension is suggested by the behavior of either Jesus or Mary— on the contrary, in fact. In contrast to Mary, Judas appears to voice a personal concern for the poor, but the narrator assures us that this is not his real interest, which is theft (12:6). Judas is no longer an intimate of Jesus, for he has become "the one about to betray him" (12:4).

Jn 20: 1,11–18 also evidences correspondence with these suggested characteristics of intimacy. It begins when Mary suddenly recognizes Jesus (20:16) and "turns" to her former relationship with him. Such a relationship would include moving close to him and touching him (20:17). The resurrected Jesus seems to remain in a more formal or guarded stance, telling Mary Magdalene to stop touching him. Jesus is apparently unable to resume the intimacy Mary assumes they share. Again, the allusions to the Song emphasize the expectation of intimate gesture, reminding the reader that the woman seeking her beloved presumes "access to the personal sphere" when she finds him.

A person in intimate relationship does not need to stop to consider his or her next move in regard to the other. Hesitation suggests doubt about the reciprocity of the connection, or concern about the appropriateness of the gesture. Persons who love each other behave candidly and immediately. Even peculiar behavior may be offered. Spontaneity indicates a move in the direction of intimacy. Mary of Bethany's unannounced extravagant gesture (Jn 12:3) appears to be impulsive, the spontaneous action of an intimate. How or why she acquired the jar of ointment is not said; perhaps it was left from Lazarus' burial and Mary abruptly decided on this use for it. In any case, the gesture is accomplished with no hesitation, indicating confidence of its acceptance, which Jesus clearly exhibits (12:7). Judas, who is not an intimate, objects vigorously to Mary's action (and, one suspects, to Mary's relationship with Jesus). He favors hesitation, planning, and finally a formal gesture toward the public realm, the poor (12:4–5). Jesus sides with spontaneity, with taking advantage of the opportunity to demonstrate love while the occasion persists (12:7–8).

Spontaneity is more subtly presented in Jn 20, beginning with Mary Magdalene's decision to go to Jesus' tomb in the dark by herself (20:1). She looks into the tomb (20:11) and does not balk at responding to the angels' and then to Jesus' questions. Her only difficulty is in not knowing she is in the intimate realm because she does not recognize her friend. The moment she does so, she calls him an affectionate name and apparently touches him (Jn 20:16b–17a). The woman in the Song, seeking her beloved, encounters outsiders (watchmen) who cause her to hesitate. As she gets past them, she meets the object of her persistent search and seizes him (SS 3:4). Throughout the Song spontaneity is invited, from the opening verse (SS 1:2, "let him kiss me") to the last (SS 8:14, "hurry, my love"). The reader who is aware of the allusive metonymy the Evangelist evokes here knows that the Song is the backdrop for much of the Magdalene-Jesus encounter and can therefore perceive its subtlety of expression.

Intimates candidly share their evaluations with each other, taking the chance that what they think will be received without judgment. In the anointing scene, only a non-intimate makes a judgment about Mary's gesture. Judas' unsolicited analysis is negative (12:5). Jesus, who had previously withheld judgment because no judgment was called for, now evaluates his friend's action positively in spite of its controversial nature (12:7). However, even an intimate may occasionally refuse familiar contact or conversation. Just so, Jesus tells Mary Magdalene that she cannot touch him; he does not explain why, but instead seems to change the subject (20:17). Jesus abruptly announces that he is not available because he has not yet gone up to his father. His demurrer comes as a surprise to the reader who expects a continuation of the move toward re-established intimacy. The allusion to the Song at this juncture recalls the woman lover's desire to bring her beloved into her mother's house and gives Jesus' startling words an ironic effect for those who are aware of the allusion.

In this chapter I began by raising questions about the social location of the Johannine community. My chief concern was whether it was likely that the Fourth Evangelist would have alluded to the Song of Songs given the community's social context. Recent scholarship reveals a virtual consensus about the separatist/sectarian nature of the Fourth Gospel community, as well as its tendency to dichotomize flesh and spirit. By referring to the sociolinguistic studies of B. J. Malina and J. H. Neyrey, the study avoids a reductionist analysis of language in isolation. Neyrey shows that the Johannine community's development of a high Christology and its increasingly dualistic esteem for spirit over flesh are in proportion to the community's growing sense of separation from "the world" and from other Christian groups. His findings about the later Johannine community contrast with my detection of a notably low Christology in the Johannine narratives that allude to the Song. This low Christology stresses the human qualities of Jesus, with little or no indication of the divinity claimed for him in so much of the Fourth Gospel.

Neyrey's evidence about the Johannine community's move from low to high Christology suggests that Jn 12:1–8 and 20:1,11–18 reflect an early stratum of that community's experience. During this period prominent community members embraced earthly experience, including friendship, the life of the senses, and the bonds of ordinary human attachment. The allusions to the Song in these texts underscore the worth of human bodily experience. The bodily and emotional realms are traditionally (perhaps stereotypically) consigned to women more than to men, and study of the Song of Songs affirms the significant influence of women on that text. Women are the prominent figures in Jn 12:1–8 and 20:1,11–18, and the community members originally responsible for these anointing and appearance narratives were very probably women.

After my inquiry about the social and theological benefits of the Johannine allusions to a text like the Song, I described speech accommodation theory and showed that the Fourth Evangelist's use of Song allusions was an element in the author's overall desire to converge with the language valued by the audience. I then explored Malina's study of the antisocietal nature of the Johannine group and their use of antilanguage to reinforce their own identity and to differentiate themselves from outsiders. I showed that the allusions to the Song in Jn 12 and 20 functioned as antilanguage, underscoring particular group values for insiders, and creating a reinforcing atmosphere for group members because of their immediate recognition of the evoked text.

Finally, I invoked an analysis of relative degrees of intimacy expressed in human relationships. I wanted to arrive at a more objective assessment of the amount and type of intimacy expressed in Jn 12:1–8 and 20:1,11–18 and also of the function of the allusions to the Song in supporting such expression. I concluded that both Fourth Gospel texts communicate an overwhelming move in the direction of intimacy between Jesus and Mary of Bethany and between Jesus and Mary Magdalene, and that the allusions to the Song of Songs in these texts contribute significantly to the prevailing atmosphere of intimate interpersonal communication.

Notes

1 See M. A. K. Halliday, "Anti-Languages," *American Anthropologist* 78 (1976): 570–584.

2 B. J. Malina, "The Gospel of Jn in Sociolinguistic Perspective," *Protocol of the Forty-eighth Colloquy*, ed. H. C. Waetjen. Berkeley: Center for Hermeneutical Studies, 1985.

3 See W. A. Meeks, "The Man from Heaven in Johannine Sectarianism," *Journal of Biblical Literature* 91 (1972): 44; Rudolf Bultmann, *The Gospel of Jn: A Commentary*, trans. G. R. Beasley-Murray (Philadelphia: Westminster Press, 1975); J. L. Martyn, *History and Theology in the Fourth Gospel* (Nashville: Abingdon, 1979); R. E. Brown, "The Qumran Scrolls and the Johannine Gospel and Epistles," *Catholic Biblical Quarterly* 17 (1955): 403–419 (part one), 559–574 (part two) and *The Community of the Beloved Disciple*.

4 Malina describes the attitudes of members of the weak group/low grid quadrant in regard to specific issues as follows:

Purity: against the purity postures of the quadrant from which it emerged.
Rite: against the rites of the quadrant from which it emerged; effervescent; spontaneity valued.
Personal identity: no antagonism between society and the self; but the old society of the quadrant from which it derived is seen as oppressive; roles of previous quadrant are rejected; self-control and/or social control are low; highly individualistic.
Body: irrelevant; life is spiritual; purity concerns are absent, but they may be rejected; body may be used freely or renunciation may prevail.
Sin: a matter of personal ethics and interiority.
Cosmology: the cosmos is likely to be impersonal; there is individual and direct access to the divinity, usually without mediation; cosmos is benign.
Suffering and Misfortune: love conquers all; love can eliminate.

(*Christian Origins and Cultural Anthropology* [Atlanta: Jn Knox Press, 1986], 14).

5 Malina, "The Gospel of Jn in Sociolinguistic Perspective," 3. Malina sees the Synoptic Gospels as satiric tragedies.

6 J. H. Neyrey, *An Ideology of Revolt* (Philadelphia: Fortress Press, 1988), 3.

7 Malina refers to "(1) soundings/spellings that (2) realize wordings that (3) realize meanings. The soundings and spellings are quite concrete; they are in fact the only dimension of language that affects the senses. The next level, wording, is about patterning soundings and spellings. Wording patterns range from textual forms, through sentence forms, to word forms. The third level, mean-

ing, is the socially significant feature expressed and realized by means of wording, which is realized by means of sounding and spelling. Given the experience of human beings as essentially social beings, those meanings come from
and in fact constitute the social system" ("John's: the Maverick Christian
Group—the Evidence of Sociolinguistics," *Biblical Theology Bulletin* 24
[1994]: 167).

8   Ibid.

9   According to Malina, "Considerate authors take their audience into account,
just like considerate conversation partners. Authors develop their scenarios
with a view to having an effect on their readers and/or listeners. There can be
little doubt that the author of Jn . . . accommodated his language to his
audience. This means that he did not invent or create his own distinctive
language characteristics" ("John's: the Maverick Christian Group," 168).

10   According to H. Giles et al., "Convergence has been defined as a linguistic
strategy whereby individuals adapt to each other's speech by means of a wide
range of linguistic features, including speech rates, pauses and utterance length,
pronunciation and so on. Divergence refers to the way in which speakers
accentuate vocal differences between themselves and others. Both of these
linguistic shifts may be either *upward* or *downward*, where the former refers
to a shift in a societally valued direction and the latter refers to modifications
toward more stigmatized forms" ("Speech Accommodation Theory: The First
Decade and Beyond," *Communication Yearbook* 10, ed. M. L. McLaughlin
[Beverly Hills, CA: Sage, 1987]: 14).

11   Malina, "John's: the Maverick Christian Group," 168.

12   Ibid.

13   M. A. K. Halliday, "Anti-Languages," 570.

14   Ibid. Halliday goes on, "An anti-language is not only parallel to an anti-society; it is in fact generated by it. . . . An anti-language stands to an anti-society
in much the same relation as does a language to a society."

15   Ibid., 576.

16   "that you may continue to believe that Jesus is the Messiah, the Son of God,
and that believing you may have life in his name"—see Malina, "John's: The
Maverick Christian Group," 174.

17   Ibid., 175.

18   P. L. Berger and T. Luckmann, *The Social Construction of Reality* (New
York: Doubleday, 1966), 172.

19   Halliday says that the metaphorical character defines the antilanguage: "an
anti-language is a metaphor for an everyday language; and this metaphorical
quality appears all the way up and down the system" ("Anti-Languages," 578).

20 M. L. Knapp catalogues how persons move toward or away from intimacy. The movement towards more intimacy is characterized by communication that is *broad, unique, efficient, flexible, smooth, personal, spontaneous,* and in which *overt judgment* is offered. Less intimacy is characterized, on the contrary, by communication that is *narrow, stylized, rigid, awkward, public, hesitant,* and *suspending overt judgment* (*Interpersonal Communication and Human Relationships,* [Boston: Allyn & Bacon, 1984]: 13–23).

Conclusion

Enigmatic elements of two Johannine narratives have confounded generations of readers. Several provocative incongruities in these stories invited our attention and precipitated a search for an explanation. The account of Mary of Bethany's unusual, and surely unexpected, use of her hair to wipe ointment on Jesus' feet (Jn 12:3) prompted the quest for a clearer sense of that text's meaning. Mary Magdalene's unexplained double turning during her encounter with the risen Jesus (Jn 20:14 and 16) made realistic assessment of her posture difficult and verged on the ludicrous. Jesus' directive that Mary Magdalene not touch (or hold) him is a non sequitur since no physical contact has been recounted, and it suggests that the reader has missed something. The initial dilemma was how to approach the enigmas so that they might be persuaded to disclose their secrets, secrets that remained veiled in spite of centuries of inquiry. The analyses of these texts provided by other interpreters opened some avenues of investigation, located several dead ends, and occasionally hinted at a few of the clues I took up. But they did not finally provide a satisfying explanation of the puzzling texts.

The challenge was straightforward: to account for words and gestures which were not incomprehensible, but which were inconsistent in their context. The pursuit of fresh solutions to old textual difficulties started with a search for appropriate tools. The inquiry about Johannine enigmas began with an elementary assumption, that the Fourth Evangelist wanted to proclaim an essential, life-giving message, as indicated in the summary statement of the Gospel (Jn 20:31). Considering the profound nature of Gospel's purpose, it seemed probable that the Evangelist would not write nonsense, but would want to be understood. Where portions of the Fourth Gospel appeared unintelligible or absurd, it was reasonable to assume that the reader was missing something that the original audience had understood. Approaching the two Johannine texts at the simplest level, as stories, I conjectured that clues about stories are often found in other stories. Because it is customary in Scripture to recount stories that have distinct intertextual antecedents in earlier narratives, it is reasonable to seek such clues. The analyses of narrative intertextuality provided by literary theorists Z. Ben-Porat and M. Riffaterre offer useful methods for this investigation, since the Johannine narratives extend intertextual tentacles similar to those that are common in other works of literature. Application of Ben-Porat's and Riffaterre's studies to the Johannine pericopes made clear that the apparently troublesome texts were intended to guide readers to perceive intertextual hints. In discovering where the hints pointed, I noted that textual signs are supported by an intuitive "readerly common sense" and an instinctive awareness of the kinds of texts that might have influenced the Johannine community. Intertextual clues led to the conclusion that the text evoked by the Johannine allusions was the Song of Songs, that, indeed, the Song of Songs is the literary matrix for these Johannine narratives. The themes, motifs, and vocabulary of the Song exhibit a remarkable similarity to those that pervade John 12:1–8 and 20:11–18, and the Song's main characters are also a woman and a man in intimate loving relationship. Investigation of *key words* (such as hair, king, voice, feet, or the many references to scent and ointment); *motifs* (such as the garden setting, the woman's turning, the mother's house); and *themes* (such as reciprocity between the beloved woman and man, their spontaneous physical contact, and their delight in each other) confirmed this suspicion. The original hypothesis is corroborated by the unusual assertiveness of the female protagonist in both the Song and the Johannine texts, as well as the preponderance of female speech and the overwhelming literary correlation between the Song and John 12 and 20.

Once the evoked text became apparent through a literary investigation, the initial perspective of the inquiry enlarged, and the intent of the analysis broadened, expanding a spiraling upward movement. The question became why—for the Evangelist and the Johannine community—the Song was, of all the possible choices, an appropriate referent text. Assessment of predominant opinion about the social context of the Johannine community led to the discovery that the community's internal focus and sense of separation from both the world and other

Christians accentuated their concern for uniqueness and individualism, their reliance on their own group, and their lack of interest in
external social structures. Johannine Christians perceived themselves
as uniquely related to Jesus and considered their relationship with him
and with each other privileged and exclusive. Their regard for intimate interpersonal bonds (that is, love) and their distinctive speech
and body language underscored their interior focus and their appre-
ciation of emotional and spiritual experience. An emphasis on the
affective and corporeal realms especially distinguishes the pericopes
studied here. In addition, the Fourth Gospel underscores the equality
and reciprocity of both male and female believers, mutual regard for
the other, and the authority of women: these qualities are especially
evident in John 12 and 20. A referent text that supports the perspective of the Johannine community would uphold these values, and,
indeed, the Song does so unequivocally. It became apparent that the
Song would have been fittingly evoked by the Fourth Evangelist. Application of B. J. Malina's adaptations of theories of speech accommodation and the language of intimacy confirms the social appropriateness of allusions to the Song.

In these final pages the focus shifts toward the ramifications of the
Johannine allusions and the opportunities suggested for further inquiry. The allusions to the Song in two chapters of the Fourth Gospel
raise the possibility that other such allusions may be found in that
Gospel. A conspicuous next step would include a fresh investigation
of the account of the raising of Lazarus (Jn 11:1–44), a story that
involves the same Bethany family as Jn 12. The Lazarus story's reference to the anointing (11:2) specifically mentions Mary's wiping Jesus'
feet with her hair. The story also describes a profound experience of
human friendship and emotion and Jesus' feelings about the Bethany
family. Other issues that invite speculation include the prominence of
female characters in both the Johannine and Song texts, and the emphasis on women figures and female experience. This element was
briefly considered, but the area invites more detailed investigation.
Further inquiry might also include an analysis of the oral stratum of
the Fourth Gospel in which the influence of women may have been
prominent. There remains also the question of the authorship of Jn
12:1–8 and Jn 20:1,11–18 and the Song, with the intriguing hint
that a similar constituency may have influenced both the Fourth Gospel and Song texts. If the *evoked* text is also influenced by the allusive
relationship, it could be profitable to consider the Fourth Gospel's

influence on subsequent Christian readings of the Song. An additional area of investigation is the role of the Song of Songs among both Jews and Christians in the first century C.E., and examination of the Song's influence on Christian liturgical practice.

Finally, the study's systematic demonstration of the allusive connections between Jn 12:1–8 and 20:1,11–18 and the Song of Songs shows that the Fourth Evangelist's methodical actuation of allusions to the Song evoked a metonymic relationship between the Fourth Gospel and the Song of Songs. Allusions to the Song contribute significantly to the articulation of the intimate relationship that some Johannine community members experienced with Jesus, and they also reinforce the community's expression of a counter-cultural perspective. The study offers a compelling interpretation of Johannine enigmas whose explanation was hidden within the texts themselves and revealed when the allusive key was discovered.

In the end, we return to the matrix. The study has focused on the literary matrix that the Song of Songs provided for the Fourth Gospel. But this evoked text also reveals a *spiritual* matrix that informed those Johannine community members who were chiefly responsible for composing and originally telling the anointing and resurrection appearance stories studied here. The spirituality of these community members, which is suggested by their affection for the Song, provides an intriguing invitation to continued investigation.

Bibliography

Alter, Robert. *The Art of Biblical Narrative*. New York: Basic Books, 1981.

————. "The Garden of Metaphor." Chap. in *The Art of Biblical Poetry*. New York: Basic Books, 1985.

————. *The Pleasures of Reading*. New York: Simon and Schuster, 1989.

————. *The World of Biblical Literature*. New York: Basic Books, 1992.

Ashton, John. *Understanding the Fourth Gospel*. Oxford: Clarendon Press, 1991.

Baarda, T. "'She Recognized Him': Concerning the Origin of a Peculiar Textual Variation in John 20,16 Sy^s." In *Text and Testimony*, ed. T. Baarda, A. Hilhorst, G. P. Luttikhuizen, and A. S. van der Woude, 24-38. Kampen: Uitgeversmaatschappij J. H. Kok, 1988.

Bal, Mieke. *Lethal Love: Feminist Literary Readings of Biblical Love Stories*. Bloomington: Indiana University Press, 1987.

Barr, James. *Holy Scripture: Canon, Authority, Criticism*. Oxford: Clarendon Press, 1983.

————. "The Literal, the Allegorical, and Modern Biblical Scholarship." *Journal for the Study of the Old Testament* 44 (1989): 3-17.

Barthès, R., P. Beauchamp, H. Bouillard, J. Courtès, E. Haulotte, X. Léon-Dufour. *Exégèse et herméneutique*. Paris: Éditions du Seuil, 1971.

Bekkenkamp, J. and F. van Dijk. "The Canon of the Old Testament and Women's Cultural Traditions." In *A Feminist Companion to the Song of Songs*, ed. A. Brenner, 67-85. Sheffield: Sheffield Academic Press, 1993.

Benages, Nuria Calduch. "La Fragrancia del Perfume en Jn 12,3," *Estudios Biblicos* 48 (1990): 243-265.

Ben-Porat, Ziva. "Disguised Wrath and Hidden Heresy: On Bialik's 'Dance of Despair'." *Prooftexts* 6 (1986): 221-237.

―――. "Forms of Intertextuality and the Reading of Poetry: Uri Zvi Greenberg's *Basha'ar*." *Prooftexts* 10 (1990): 257–281.

―――. *The Poetics of Allusion*. Ph.D. diss., University of California at Berkeley, 1973.

―――. "The Poetics of Literary Allusion." *PTL: A Journal for Descriptive Poetics and Theory of Literature* 1 (1976): 105–128.

Berger, P. L. and T. Luckmann. *The Social Construction of Reality*. Garden City, NY: Doubleday & Company, 1966.

Bernabé, C. "Trasfondo Derásico de Jn 20," *Estudios Biblicos* 49 (1991): 209–228.

Bloch, Ariel and Chana Bloch. *The Song of Songs*. New York: Random House, 1995.

Boyarin, Daniel. "Inner Biblical Ambiguity, Intertextuality and the Dialectic of Midrash: The Waters of Marah." *Prooftexts* 10 (1990): 29–48.

―――. *Intertextuality and the Reading of Midrash*. Bloomington: Indiana University Press, 1990.

―――. "The Song of Songs: Lock or Key? Intertextuality, Allegory and Midrash." In *The Book and the Text*, ed. R. M. Schwartz, 214–230. Cambridge: Basil Blackwell, Inc., 1990.

Brenner, Athalya. "'Come Back, Come Back the Shulammite' (Song of Songs 7.1-10): A Parody of the *Wasf* Genre." In *On Humour and the Comic in the Hebrew Bible*, ed. Y. T. Radday and A. Brenner, 251–275. Sheffield: The Almond Press, 1990.

―――, ed. *A Feminist Companion to the Song of Songs*. Sheffield: Sheffield Academic Press, 1993.

————. *The Israelite Woman: Social Role and Literary Type in Biblical Narrative*. Sheffield: JSOT Press, 1985.

————. *The Song of Songs*, Old Testament Guides series. Sheffield: JSOT Press, 1989.

Brenner, A. and F. van Dijk-Hemmes. *On Gendering Texts: Female and Male Voices in the Hebrew Bible*. Leiden: E. J. Brill, 1993.

Brésard , L. and H. Crouzel. *Origen's Commentaire sur le Cantique des Cantiques,* Tome II, Sources Chrétiennes 376. Paris: Éditions du Cerf, 1992.

Brown, R. E. *The Churches the Apostles Left Behind*. New York: Paulist Press, 1984.

————. *The Community of the Beloved Disciple*. New York: Paulist Press, 1979.

————. *The Gospel according to John (i-xii)*. Anchor Bible 29. Garden City, NY: Doubleday & Co., 1966.

————. *The Gospel according to John (xiii-xxi)*. Anchor Bible 29A. Garden City, NY: Doubleday & Co., 1970.

————. "The Qumran Scrolls and the Johannine Gospel and Epistles." *Catholic Biblical Quarterly* 17 (1955): 403-419 (part one), 559–574 (part two).

Bruns, Gerald L. *Hermeneutics Ancient and Modern*. New Haven: Yale University Press, 1992.

————. *Inventions: Writing, Textuality, and Understanding in Literary History*. New Haven: Yale University Press, 1982.

————. "Midrash and Allegory: the Beginnings of Scriptural Interpretation." In *The Literary Guide to the Bible*, edited by R. Alter and F. Kermode, 625–647. Cambridge: Harvard University Press, 1990.

Bruns, J. E. "A Note on John 12,3." *Catholic Biblical Quarterly* 28 (1966): 219–222.

Bultmann, Rudolf. *The Gospel of Jn: A Commentary*. Translated by G. R. Beasley-Murray. Philadelphia: Westminster Press, 1975.

Buss, M. J. "Hosea as a Canonical Problem: With Attention to the Song of Songs." In *Prophets and Paradigms*, edited by S. B.

Reid, 79–93. JSOT Supplement Series 229. Sheffield: Sheffield Academic Press, 1996.

Cambe, M. "L'influence du Cantique des Cantiques sur le Nouveau Testament." *Revue Thomiste* 62 (1962): 5–25.

Carson, D. A. "Current Source Criticism of the Fourth Gospel: some methodological questions." *Journal of Biblical Literature* 97 (1978): 411–429.

Carson, D. A. and H. G. M. Williamson, eds. *It Is Written: Scripture Citing Scripture.* Cambridge: Cambridge University Press, 1988.

Carson, D. A. and J. D. Woodbridge, eds. *Hermeneutics, Authority, and Canon.* Grand Rapids: Zondervan, 1986.

Cassidy, R. J. *John's Gospel in New Perspective.* Maryknoll, NY: Orbis Books, 1992.

Coakley, J. F. "The Anointing at Bethany and the Priority of John," *Journal of Biblical Literature* 107/2 (1988): 241–256.

Corley, Kathleen E. *Private Women, Public Meals: Social Conflict in the Synoptic Tradition.* Peabody, MA: Hendrickson Publishers, 1993.

Culler, Jonathan. *The Pursuit of Signs: Semiotics,Literature, Deconstruction.* Ithaca, NY: Cornell University Press, 1981.

———. *Structuralist Poetics.* London: Routledge and Kegan Paul, 1975.

Culpepper, R. A. *Anatomy of the Fourth Gospel.* Philadelphia: Fortress Press, 1983.

———. *The Johannine School.* Missoula: Scholars Press, 1975.

D'Angelo, M. R. "A Critical Note: Jn 20:17 and Apocalypse of Moses 31." *Journal of Theological Studies* 41 (1990): 529–536.

Davies, Margaret. *Rhetoric and Reference in the Fourth Gospel.* Sheffield: JSOT Press, 1992.

Davies, W. D. "Reflections about the Use of the Old Testament in the New in its Historical Context." *The Jewish Quarterly Review* 74 (1983): 105–136.

Daube, D. "The Anointing at Bethany and Jesus' Burial." *Anglican Theological Review* 32 (1950): 186–199.

Dillon, R. "Wisdom Tradition and Sacramental Retrospect in the Cana Account." *Catholic Biblical Quarterly* 24 (1962): 268–296.

Draisma, Sipke, ed. *Intertextuality in Biblical Writings*. Kampen: Uitgeversmaatschappij J. H. Kok, 1989.

Duke, Paul. *Irony in the Fourth Gospel*. Atlanta: John Knox Press, 1985.

Elliott, J. K. "The Anointing of Jesus." *The Expository Times* 85 (1974): 105–107.

Eslinger, Lyle. "Inner-Biblical Exegesis and Inner-Biblical Allusion: The Question of Category." *Vetus Testamentus* 42:1 (1992): 47–58.

Evans, Craig A. "Obduracy and the Lord's Servant: Some Observations on the Use of the Old Testament in the Fourth Gospel." In *Early Jewish and Christian Exegesis*, ed. C. A. Evans and W. F. Stinespring, 221–236. Atlanta: Scholars Press, 1987.

Exum, J. Cheryl and D. J. A. Clines. *The New Literary Criticism and the Hebrew Bible*. Sheffield: Sheffield Academic Press, 1993.

Falk, Marcia. *The Song of Songs*. San Francisco: HarperCollins, 1990.

Feuillet, A. "Les deux onctions faites sur Jésus, et Marie-Madeleine." *Revue Thomiste* 75 (1975): 353–394.

———. "La formule d'appartenance mutuelle (II,16) et les interprétations divergentes du Cantique des Cantiques." *Revue Biblique* 68 (1961): 5–38.

———. "La recherche du Christ dans la Nouvelle Alliance d'après la Christophanie de Jo. 20, 11–18." In *L'Homme devant Dieu* (Mélanges offerts au père Henri de Lubac), 93–112. Paris: Aubier, 1963.

Fewell, Danna N., ed. *Reading Between Texts: Intertextuality and the Hebrew Bible*. Louisville, Kentucky: Westminster/John Knox Press, 1992.

Fishbane, Michael. "Interpretation of Mikra at Qumran." In *Mikra: Text, Translation, Reading and Interpretation of the Hebrew Bible in Ancient Judaism and Early Christianity*, ed. M. J. Mulder, 339–377. Philadelphia: Fortress Press, 1988.

————. "The Qumran Pesher and Traits of Ancient Hermeneutics." In *Proceedings of the Sixth World Congress of Jewish Studies 1*. Jerusalem, 1977: 97–114.

Fortna, Robert. *The Gospel of Signs*. Cambridge: Cambridge University Press, 1970.

————. *The Fourth Gospel and its Predecessor*. Philadelphia: Fortress Press, 1988.

Fox, Michael V. *The Song of Songs and the Ancient Egyptian Love Songs*. Madison: University of Wisconsin Press, 1985.

Freed, Edwin D. *Old Testament Quotations in the Gospel of John*. Leiden: E. J. Brill, 1965.

Giblin, C. H. "Mary's Anointing for Jesus' Burial-Resurrection (John 12,1–8)." *Biblica* 73 (1992): 560–564.

Giles, H. and J. M. Wiemann. "Language, Social Comparison, and Power." In *Handbook of Communication Science*, ed. C. R. Berger and S. H. Chaffee, 350–384. Beverly Hills, CA: Sage, 1987.

Giles, H., A. Mulac, J. J. Bradac, and P. Johnson. "Speech Accommodation Theory: The First Decade and Beyond." In *Communication Yearbook* 10, ed. M. L. McLaughlin, 13–48.

Beverly Hills, CA: Sage, 1987.

Ginsburg, C. D. *The Song of Songs and Qoheleth*. New York: KTAV Publishing House, 1970 (1857).

Goitein, S. D. "Women as Creators of Biblical Genres." *Prooftexts 8* (1988): 1–33.

Goodenough, E. R. "John, a Primitive Gospel." *Journal of Biblical Literature* 64 (1945): 145–182.

Gottwald, N. K. "The Song of Songs." Chap. in *The Hebrew Bible: A Socio-Literary Introduction*. Philadelphia: Fortress Press, 1985.

Grant, R. M. "Literary Criticism and the New Testament Canon." *Journal for the Study of the New Testament* 16 (1982): 22–44.

Halivni, David Weiss. *Peshat and Derash: Plain and Applied Meaning in Rabbinic Exegesis*. New York: Oxford University Press, 1991.

Halliday, M. A. K. "Anti-Languages." *American Anthropologist* 78 (1976): 570–584.

———. *Language as Social Semiotic.* London: Edward Arnold, Ltd., 1978.

Hanson, Anthony T. *The New Testament Interpretation of Scripture.* London: SPCK, 1980.

———. *The Prophetic Gospel: a Study of John and the Old Testament.* Edinburgh: T&T Clark, 1991.

Hengel, M. *The Johannine Question.* Translated by J. Bowden. London: SCM Press, 1989.

Holladay, W. L. *The Root Subh in the Old Testament.* Leiden: E. J. Brill, 1958.

Holst, R. "The One Anointing of Jesus: another Application of the Form-Critical Method." *Journal of Biblical Literature* 95 (1976): 435–446.

Jeremias, Joachim. *The Parables of Jesus.* London: SCM Press, 1963.

Johns, Loren L. and Douglas B. Miller. "The Signs as Witnesses in the Fourth Gospel." *Catholic Biblical Quarterly* 56 (1994): 519–535.

Juel, Donald. *Messianic Exegesis.* Philadelphia: Fortress Press, 1988.

Keel, Othmar. *The Song of Songs.* Translated by F. J. Gaiser. Minneapolis: Fortress Press, 1994.

Kitzberger, Ingrid Rosa. "Mary of Bethany and Mary of Magdala—Two Female Characters in the Johannine Passion Narrative." *New Testament Studies* 41 (1995): 564–586.

Knapp, M. L. *Interpersonal Communication and Human Relationships.* Boston: Allyn & Bacon, 1984.

Kronfeld, Chana. "Allusion: An Israeli Perspective." *Prooftexts* 5 (1985): 137–163.

Kugel, James L. Review of *Biblical Interpretation in Early Israel* by Michael Fishbane. *Prooftexts* 7 (1987): 269–305.

Kugel, James L. and Rowan A. Greer. *Early Biblical Interpretation.* Philadelphia: Westminster, 1986.

Lagrange, M.-J. "Jésus a-t-il été oint plusieurs fois et par plusieurs femmes?" *Revue Biblique* 9 (1912): 504–532.

Legault, A. "An Application of the Form-Critique Method to the Anointings in Galilee (Lk 7:36–50), and Bethany (Mt 26:6-13, Mk 14:3–9, Jn 12:1–8)." *Catholic Biblical Quarterly* 16 (1954): 131–145.

Longenecker, Richard N. "Three Ways of Understanding Relations between the Testaments—historically and today." In *Tradition and Interpretation in the New Testament*, ed. G. F. Hawthorne and O. Betz, 22–32. Grand Rapids: Eerdmans, 1987.

Malina, Bruce. *Christian Origins and Cultural Anthropology: Practical Models for Biblical Interpretation*. Atlanta: John Knox Press, 1986.

———. *The Gospel of John in Sociolinguistic Perspective: Protocol of the forty-eighth colloquy*, edited by H. C. Waetjen. Berkeley: Center for Hermeneutical Studies, 1985.

———. "John's: the Maverick Christian Group—the Evidence of Sociolinguistics." *Biblical Theology Bulletin* 24 (1994): 167–182.

———. *The New Testament World: Insights from Cultural Anthropology*. Atlanta: John Knox Press, 1981.

Mariaselvam, A. *The Song of Songs and Ancient Tamil Love Poems*. Rome: Editrice Pontifico Istituto Biblico, 1988.

Martyn, J. L. *History and Theology in the Fourth Gospel*. Nashville: Abingdon, 1979.

McGinn, Bernard. "With the Kisses of His Mouth: Recent Works on the Song of Songs." *Journal of Religion* (1992): 269–275.

McKnight, E. V. and E. S. Malbon. *The New Literary Criticism and the New Testament*. Valley Forge, PA: Trinity Press International, 1994.

Meeks, W. A. "Breaking Away: Three New Testament Pictures of Christianity's Separation from the Jewish Communities." In *To See Ourselves as Others See Us: Christians, Jews, "Others" in Late Antiquity*, edited by J. Neusner and E. S. Frerichs, 93–115. Chico, CA: Scholars Press, 1985.

————. "The Man from Heaven in Johannine Sectarianism." *Journal of Biblical Literature* 91 (1972): 44–72.

————. *The Prophet King: Moses Traditions and Johannine Christology.* Leiden: E. J. Brill, 1967.

Meloni, P. *Il Profumo dell'Immortalità: l'interpretazione patristica di Cantico 1,3.* Rome: Edizioni Studium, 1975.

Meyers, Carol. "Gender Imagery in the Song of Songs." *Hebrew Annual Review* 10 (1986): 209–223.

Murphy, Roland E. "Patristic and Medieval Exegesis—Help or Hindrance?" *Catholic Biblical Quarterly* 43 (1981): 505–516.

————. "Old Testament/Tanakh—Canon and Interpretation." In *Hebrew Bible or Old Testament?* ed. R. Brooks and J. Collins, 11–29. Notre Dame: University of Notre Dame Press, 1990.

————. *The Song of Songs.* Minneapolis: Fortress Press, 1990.

Neusner, Jacob. *Song of Songs Rabbah: an analytical translation* (vols. 1 & 2). Atlanta: Scholars Press, 1989.

————. *Canon and Connection.* Lanham, MD: University Press of America, 1987.

Neyrey, Jerome H. "The Christologies of John's Gospel." Chap. in *Christ Is Community: the Christologies of the New Testament.* Wilmington, DL: Michael Glazier, 1985.

————. *An Ideology of Revolt: John's Christology in Social-Science Perspective.* Philadelphia: Fortress Press, 1988.

O'Day, Gail R. "Jeremiah 9:22-23 and 1 Corinthians 1:26-31: A Study in Intertextuality." *Journal of Biblical Literature* 109 (1990): 259–267.

————. *Revelation in the Fourth Gospel.* Philadelphia: Fortress Press, 1986.

Patterson, L. *Negotiating the Past.* Madison: University of Wisconsin Press, 1987.

Pope, Marvin H. "Metastases in Canonical Shapes of the Super Song." In *Canon, Theology, and Old Testament Interpretation,* ed. G. M. Tucker, D. L. Petersen, and R. R. Wilson, 312–328. Philadelphia: Fortress Press, 1988:.

————. *Song of Songs*, Anchor Bible series 7C. New York: Doubleday, 1977.

Prete, B. "Un' Aporia giovannea: il testo di Giov. 12,3." *Rivista Biblica Italiana* 25 (1977): 357–374.

Ricoeur, Paul. *Le conflit des interprétations: essais d'herméneutique.* Paris: Éditions du Seuil, 1969.

————. "La fonction herméneutique de la distanciation." In *Exegesis: problèmes de méthode et exercices de lecture,* ed. F. Bovon and G. Rouiller, 201–215. Paris: Delachaux et Niestlé, 1975.

————. "Herméneutique philosophique et herméneutique biblique." In *Exegesis: problèmes de méthode et exercices de lecture,* ed. F. Bovon and G. Rouiller, 216–228. Paris: Delachaux et Niestlé, 1975.

————. *Interpretation Theory.* Fort Worth, TX: Texas Christian University Press, 1976.

————. "La tâche de l'herméneutique." In *Exegesis: problèmes de méthode et exercices de lecture,* ed. F. Bovon and G. Rouiller, 179–200. Paris: Delachaux et Niestlé, 1975.

Ricoeur, Paul, Emmanuel Levinas, Edgar Haulotte, Etienne Cornelis, Claude Geffre. *La révélation.* Bruxelles: Facultés universitaires Saint-Louis, 1977.

Riffaterre, Michel. *Fictional Truth.* Baltimore: The Johns Hopkins University Press, 1990.

————. *Semiotics of Poetry.* Bloomington, IN: Indiana University Press, 1978.

Rogers, E. M. *Diffusion of Innovations.* New York: The Free Press, 1983.

Sabbe, M. "The Anointing of Jesus in John 12,1-8 and its Synoptic Parallels." In *The Four Gospels*, ed. F. Van Segbroek, C. M. Tuckett, G. Van Belle, and J. Verheyden, vol. 3, 2051–2082. Leuven: Leuven University Press, 1992.

Sanders, J. N. "Those Whom Jesus Loved (John XI,5)." *New Testament Studies* I (1954-55): 29–41.

Sanders, James A. *Canon and Community.* Philadelphia: Fortress, 1984.

———. *From Sacred Story to Sacred Text*. Philadelphia: Fortress, 1987.

———. *Torah and Canon*. Philadelphia: Fortress, 1972.

Schneiders, Sandra M. "From Exegesis to Hermeneutics: the Problem of the Contemporary Meaning of Scripture." *Horizons* 8 (1981): 23–39.

———. "The Foot-Washing (John 13:1-20): an Experiment in Hermeneutics." *Catholic Biblical Quarterly* 43 (1981): 76–92.

———. "The Johannine Resurrection Narrative." S. T. D. diss. Pontificia Universitas Gregoriana, 1975.

———. "John 21:1-14." *Interpretation* 43 (1989): 70–75.

———. "The Paschal Imagination: Objectivity and Subjectivity in New Testament Interpretation." *Theological Studies* 43 (1982): 52–68.

———. *The Revelatory Text*. San Francisco: Harper, 1991.

———. "Scripture and Spirituality." In *Christian Spirituality I (Origins to the 12th Century)*, ed. B. McGinn and J. Meyendorff, 1–20. New York: Crossroad, 1985.

———. "Women in the Fourth Gospel and the Role of Women in the Contemporary Church." *Biblical Theology Bulletin* 12 (1982): 35–45.

Schüssler Fiorenza, Elisabeth. *Bread Not Stone: the Challenge of Feminist Biblical Interpretation*. Boston: Beacon Press, 1984.

———. *But She Said: Feminist Practices of Biblical Interpretation*. Boston: Beacon Press, 1992.

———. *In Memory of Her*. New York: Crossroad, 1983.

Scott, Martin. *Sophia and the Johannine Jesus*. Sheffield: JSOT Press, 1992.

Showalter, E. "Women's Writing and Women's Culture." In *The New Feminist Criticism: Essays on Women, Literature, and Theory*, ed. E. Showalter, 259–270. London: Virago, 1986.

Sibinga, J. S. "Towards Understanding the Composition of John 20." In *The Four Gospels*, ed. F. Van Segbroek, C. M. Tuckett,

G. Van Belle, and J. Verheyden, vol. 3, 2139–2152. Leuven: Leuven University Press, 1992.

Smith, D. Moody. "The Use of the Old Testament in the New," in *The Use of the Old Testament in the New and other essays*, ed. J. M. Efird Durham, NC: Duke University Press, 1972.

Steinmetz, David C. "The Superiority of Pre-Critical Exegesis." *Theology Today* 37 (1980): 27–38.

Sternberg, Meir. *The Poetics of Biblical Narrative*. Bloomington: Indiana University Press, 1985.

Stibbe, M. W. G. *John as Storyteller*. Cambridge: Cambridge University Press, 1992.

Tov, E. "The Septuagint," in *Mikra: Text, Translation, Reading and Interpretation of the Hebrew Bible in Ancient Judaism and Early Christianity*, ed. M. J. Mulder. Philadelphia: Fortress Press, 1988.

van Dijk-Hemmes, F. "The Imagination of Power and the Power of Imagination: An Intertextual Analysis of Two Biblical Love Songs: The Song of Songs and Hosea 2." *Journal for the Study of the Old Testament* 44 (1989): 75–88.

———. "Traces of Women's Texts in the Hebrew Bible." In *On Gendering Texts: Female and Male Voices in the Hebrew Bible*, ed. A. Brenner and F. van Dijk-Hemmes, 17–109. Leiden: E. J. Brill, 1993.

von Wahlde, U. C. *The Earliest Version of John's Gospel: Recovering the Gospel of Signs*. Wilmington, DL: Michael Glazier, 1989.

White, John B. *A Study of the Language of Love in the Song of Songs and Ancient Egyptian Poetry*. SBL Dissertation Series 38. Missoula: Scholars Press, 1978.

Wilcox, Max. "On Investigating the Use of the Old Testament in the New Testament." In *Text and Interpretation,* ed. E. Best and R. M. Wilson, 231–243. Cambridge: Cambridge University Press, 1979.

Witherup, Ronald D. "Modern Literary Criticism: Patristic Exegesis Revisited?" *Bulletin de Saint-Sulpice* 13 (1987): 81–90.

Wright, Addison G. *The Literary Genre Midrash.* New York: Alba House, 1967.

Wyatt, N. "'Supposing Him to Be the Gardener' (John 20:15): a Study of the Paradise Motif in John," *Zeitschrift für die Neutestamentliche Wissenschaft* 81 (1990): 21–38.

Studies in Biblical Literature

This series invites manuscripts from scholars in any area of biblical literature. Both established and innovative methodologies, covering general and particular areas in biblical study, are welcome. The series seeks to make available studies that will make a significant contribution to the ongoing biblical discourse. Scholars who have interests in gender and sociocultural hermeneutics are particularly encouraged to consider this series.

For further information about the series and for the submission of manuscripts, contact:

Hemchand Gossai
Department of Philosophy and Religion
Culver-Stockton College
Canton, MO 63435

To order other books in this series, please contact our Customer Service Department:

800-770-LANG (within the U.S.)
(212) 647-7706 (outside the U.S.)
(212) 647-7707 FAX

or browse online by series at:

WWW.PETERLANG.COM